ZERO

— TO —

100

ZERO
—— TO ——
100

THE BLOOD, SWEAT, AND TEARS OF BUILDING A FITNESS CHAIN FROM IDEA TO 100 LOCATIONS

SHANNON *The Cannon* HUDSON

OPEN BOOK EDITIONS
A Berrett-Koehler Partner

iUniverse®

ZERO TO 100
THE BLOOD, SWEAT, AND TEARS OF BUILDING A FITNESS CHAIN FROM IDEA TO 100 LOCATIONS

iUniverse books may be ordered through booksellers or by contacting:

iUniverse
1663 Liberty Drive
Bloomington, IN 47403
www.iuniverse.com
1-800-Authors (1-800-288-4677)

Because of the dynamic nature of the Internet, any web addresses or links contained in this book may have changed since publication and may no longer be valid. The views expressed in this work are solely those of the author and do not necessarily reflect the views of the publisher, and the publisher hereby disclaims any responsibility for them.

Any people depicted in stock imagery provided by Thinkstock are models, and such images are being used for illustrative purposes only. Certain stock imagery © Thinkstock.

ISBN: 978-1-4917-6547-0 (sc)
ISBN: 978-1-4917-6952-2 (hc)
ISBN: 978-1-4917-6546-3 (e)

Library of Congress Control Number: 2016900584

Printed in the USA.

iUniverse rev. date: 2/24/2016

To my two beautiful children,
Jackson Hudson and Elana Otero—
go build your empire!

CONTENTS

FOREWORD

Every now and then, someone is born who knows his or her purpose early on. Shannon Hudson is one of those people. He knew very early that he was born for leadership. He was excited by lofty goals. He got "turned on" by the thought of calculated risk and pushing the envelope. Never one to listen much to any words of caution, he is a trailblazer in the business world. The idea might have been given to many, but he is the one who acted on the idea. Action is a gift. Some people think. Others act. Shannon Hudson is one who acts.

It's not often that you find someone who could choose between two career paths—one as a professional athlete and the other as a founder of a worldwide brand. You're about to take a superbly grounded look into this choice and how it transpired. This is a story of an entrepreneur and fighter meets mentor and family man. The result is one of the most down-to-earth success stories you've ever read.

If you're a small-business owner or ever wanted to own your own business, this book is for you. If you want to know exactly what steps are needed for you to take your business to one hundred locations or you just need some inspiration to keep fighting the good fight, this book is definitely for you. *Zero to 100* will make you feel like you're talking to someone who's just like you but willing to share his secret. You'll no doubt relate to the daily situations such as making payroll, state and federal guidelines, competition, product quality, expansion, and marketing. Hopefully, you will be refreshed by the suggested solutions.

Most small-business owners are truly amazing people with real and fantastic dreams and the very best intentions. Sadly, too often these talented people fall prey to the belief that if *they* know how amazing their businesses are, so will everyone else. If only this were true. If these people only knew what is in this book, then their businesses could be saved, turned around, and thriving beyond their dreams. (That is, assuming they are willing to apply what they will read in these pages!) This book is the perfect example of a story with the basic message, "If I can do it, so can you."

There are too few courageous souls out there willing to dream big enough to be entrepreneurs, and so this book is an attempt to save and preserve the entrepreneurial spirit and encourage more people who are willing to dream big to emerge so that more businesses will flourish. The world needs more people like you, the ones holding this book, with a dream, faith, and some motivation—motivation that will grow as you read on!

Shannon Hudson has known for a long time that he "had a book in him," and, as his wife, I am so very happy to see him finally take pen to paper. I know how important sharing these real life lessons is for him. I know the real person behind these pages, and I invite you to step a little closer and enjoy the journey from zero to one hundred.

—Heather Love Hudson

ACKNOWLEDGMENTS

There are so many people I would love to thank for helping me get where I am and helping me write this book. The first and foremost is my family. My parents gave me an unbelievable start to life. I am forever grateful. I love you guys so much, and you continue to teach me by example.

I would like to thank my big brother, Kevin, for starting karate back in 1979. If it weren't for you, I would probably not be doing this today. While working together in the past, we have had our differences, but you are my one and only brother, and I love you. I will always be here for you. You continue to help me with 9Round to this day, and it's much appreciated.

I have to thank my beautiful wife, Heather. You astound me every day with your intellect and your amazing ability to balance being a mother, wife, fitness expert, and businesswoman. Thank you so much for encouraging me to write this book and all the late-night proofreading and editing sessions. Without you, this book would not make any sense at all. Thanks again for teaching me how to use a comma. I enjoy working with you and can't wait to do it again tomorrow with you beside me.

From the company side, I would like to thank Justin Hammerstrom. Your energy and work ethic brings a smile to the team every week. I have watched your leadership and teaching skills grow each month as we train new franchise owners together. I appreciate your loyalty and your talent with people. After all, we are not in the fitness business; we are in the people business. You have become fantastic at being a people person.

In the company, I would also like to thank Jeff Mathews for going through some crazy stuff during the difficult times with the 24-7 partnership. You always stayed true to yourself, always did the right thing, and always put your family first. You are a great example of a talented franchise salesman and an even better example of a husband, father, and friend. I appreciate all you have done and can't wait for you to crack a thousand sales with 9Round.

I would also like to thank Drew Brashier and Jason Bishop for seeing my vision and always giving it your best for the company. Let's keep rocking, because you guys have a very bright future ahead with 9Round.

Finally, I have to thank all the 9Round franchise partners. I want to thank you for keeping the American dream alive and owning your own business. Nothing is more rewarding than being an entrepreneur. And I would like to thank you from the bottom of my heart for believing and investing in *me*. Obviously, you saw something in me, and you put up your hard-earned cash and worked like a dog to open your 9Round location. I admire that. I know firsthand how difficult it is to open and run a successful business. Let's continue this wild ride together as we become the leading brand in the fitness industry. I give you my word that I will always do my best and will never forget what it's like to be an operator and in your shoes. Let's get your community fit, nine rounds at a time. I love you all.

Oh, and I have one more thank-you to give. That's a heartfelt thanks to *you*! I have opened my heart to you and feel as though I am running naked through the streets of life. I sincerely pray that these pages will inspire you to become a powerful CEO of your life. If you're a mother, become a powerful CEO mother. If you're a brother, become a powerful CEO brother. If you're an employee, become a powerful CEO of whatever your position is. I believe in the human race. I believe that we are all connected. I believe in a higher power that we can all tap into if we just believe. I believe in *you*. Now I have to get back to work. I have to help people get fit, nine rounds at a time.

INTRODUCTION

I've read countless biographies and memoirs, and for each, I've just never quite been able to connect with the author or the founder of the business being discussed. Although all were inspiring and some more interesting than others, there just seemed to be something missing. I finally had my aha moment when I was reading about Ray Kroc (the man who franchised McDonald's).

"What was the missing link?" you might ask. All the great founders I had read about wrote their experiences years after the companies they founded were a soaring success. Or worse, someone else wrote the story, and we (the readers) didn't get the real version from the actual creator. Just imagine stopping Leonardo da Vinci as he was painting the Mona Lisa and asking him, "What's going on here? What's her story?"

This book is *my* secret notepad for you to read. In this book, you will find what it really takes to bring an idea to reality with speed, efficiency, and creativity.

I searched and searched, read book after book, and just couldn't find anything even close to what I was looking for. I thought, *Boy, wouldn't it have been great to stumble upon some notes about Sam Walton's trials and tribulations as he went from one retail store to the first one hundred?* It wasn't just the story I sought but the lessons learned as well—and not a reflection years afterward but an account of his struggles and successes *while* he was still building the company.

There is something so real about seeing a founder's thoughts *as* he or she is building his or her business, not *after* it has been built. In fact, I know there are many others out there just like Ray Kroc, Steve Jobs, and Donald Trump, and this country needs them. Heck, the entire world needs them. These are the reasons I decided to write *Zero to 100*.

As the founder and CEO of 9Round (the world's largest kickboxing fitness chain), I wanted to give you the real story. I wanted so desperately to speak directly to *you*. I know that another one of those founders might be *you*. You might have an idea in your head that could change the world. You might just pick up one thing in this book that gives you some mental sunshine and clarity to help you go for it!

Whether you are contemplating starting your own business, purchasing a franchise, love reading self-help books, are a CEO of a billion-dollar firm, or just want to read a good story, this is as real as it gets. I have gone through a ton of twists, turns, and ups and downs to get 9Round to one hundred locations, and I tell it all right here. Only one person knows the real story, until now. I pull no punches. There's only one thing better than the truth, and that's the whole truth.

There are two ways to start a business. You can start a business from scratch, or you can purchase a franchise. Both have their pros and cons, but there are many benefits to purchasing a franchise. And in this book, you'll see my story mostly from the franchise point of view.

Investing in a franchised system is a great way to get into business and not be alone. When you are part of a network of people who share similar interests, you don't feel that you are out there on a limb and sometimes barely holding on. Starting a business from scratch involves a big learning curve that takes time and money. One of the most important benefits of a franchised system is that all the research and development has been done and the businessman or businesswoman does not have to waste time trying a new concept, maybe failing, and then trying another. A thoroughly market-tested game plan is already in place for you. If you follow it and work hard, you will prosper. If you *really* work hard at it, you will no doubt excel. With a franchised system, you'll have a network of support, with other people who are in business doing the exact same thing you are doing. You can call people and brainstorm with them. This support system is invaluable. If you go it alone, you don't have that.

Even with a franchise, there are many tiny details and lessons to be learned. These things are easy to miss, and it's important to take time and pick up a nugget or two to improve your life, whether it's through seminars, books, or reflection on your life. That's why, at the end of each chapter, I have included the "Knockout Nuggets." I don't want you to sleepwalk through life, missing all the lessons as you go. Most people *think* they're thinking, but they really aren't. Most people are just going through the motions and doing the same thing over and over—wondering why they keep getting the same results. Make sure you're noticing and soaking up every nugget of knowledge along the way.

I hope this isn't a book you just read and put aside. I hope you highlight what's important to you, make notes in the margins, and share it with your friends. Enjoy!

CHAPTER ONE

HUMBLE BEGINNINGS

When I made my grand entrance into this world in 1979, my older brother (and only sibling) Kevin started his martial arts journey. Kevin saw a talent show in which a kid performed karate, and he immediately told my mom and dad, "I want to do *that*." Always wanting to encourage us kids to follow our dreams, my parents signed Kevin up for those karate lessons. Because of that moment, many of my earliest memories revolve around karate. Of course my dad believed, like any parent of an eight-year-old would, that karate was just another childhood trend that would blow over in a month or so.

Boy, did that turn out to be a failed prediction! I don't blame Dad though. Who could have foreseen back then the profound impact the martial arts would have, not only on their oldest son but also on all of us? My parents had no idea of the life-changing effects that would follow the simple act of enrolling my brother in that class. In fact, they didn't make much out of it at all.

Naturally, as the younger brother, I looked up to Kevin. I thought everything he did was so cool. I, of course, wanted to be just like him. Ironically, however, my first athletic interest ended up being in gymnastics, not karate. As a kid who was on the smaller side and always very athletic, I loved watching gymnasts on TV, and I would mimic the gymnasts' moves, either out in the yard or right there in the living room. But I never took classes or got serious about it. Instead, inspired by my brother, at the age of seven, I finally decided to enroll in my first karate class at the Greer/Lyman School of Karate, where my brother had been attending since I was born.

I had already spent hours watching the classes from the sidelines. At that young age, I was a painfully shy kid, and I can still see myself sitting on the wall watching the classes my brother took. I would imagine being brave enough to walk up to the tape that marked off the practice area. But that was all in my imagination. My brother was really great. He would practice moves with me at home. That built my confidence up enough to think that maybe I could do it too. In fact, the only reason I ever started class was my brother's encouragement, which made me feel comfortable.

I can still remember the day of my very first karate class. The pungent smell of the dojo seemed more intense that day. Sweat and carpet just don't go together very well. I remember my first lesson with the zigzag patterned tape on the floor. Following this tape with your feet taught you to train your muscles to memorize the position called *forward stance*. It's the most elementary position, but it's where every white belt starts. We even sparred (person-to-person hitting) in my very first class. And even though it scared me, I loved it—in the way you love the thrill of a roller coaster. It was terrifying and exhilarating. Classes were on Monday, Tuesday, and Thursday from 6:00 p.m. to 8:00 p.m. The schedule is a far cry from what most karate schools do today. Three classes a week at two hours a pop is not mainstream anymore! But the discipline I learned in those days was invaluable.

The class format was the same every time, and I took to it like a fish to water. If I missed class, I always felt guilty, like maybe I had let my parents or my big brother down. When a martial arts school is as serious as the one I learned at, it teaches kids to live up to their commitments without question. I still carry this deeply engrained mantra with me every day. It's just part of who I am.

Back then, the karate instructors threw you to the wolves— sink or swim. It was a gruff atmosphere, and you had to be pretty tough yourself to even show up. The classes in the mid-1980s were made up of twenty to thirty people, which usually included only about three or four kids. I never cared then if I was the smallest one in the class. I was determined to be one of the best. Later in life when I became a business owner, I drew on this experience and the burning desire to be good at something cultivated in me at an early age.

My brother and I always had an open mind and studied other martial arts. Over the years, we have visited literally hundreds of other martial arts schools. Through those visits, we learned not only a variety of types of physical training but also the ins and outs of a range of styles for handling the business side of things. I have always been a sponge and try to learn as much as I can when I visit others. I also had the privilege to earn a fourth-degree black belt under Joe Lewis (the martial arts expert, not the boxer), who pioneered full contact kickboxing in America in the late sixties and early seventies. Lewis had trained with Bruce Lee, the famous Asian martial artist who came to America and became a movie star. He introduced incredible fight scenes to the big screen that paved the way for current action actors, such as Chuck Norris, Jackie Chan, and Jet Le. Martial arts movies like *Enter the Dragon* have become classics. Whenever that movie comes on, I still just have to watch it.

I also entered a number of tournaments, relishing in the competition every time. I love to win, and I found victory exhilarating as one trophy after another went home with me. I will never forget my first karate tournament. I was a brown belt. I got first place in kata (forms) division and second place in sparring (fighting). I remember crying after the kid beat me in sparring. I still have the trophies collecting dust in the attic, and today, my little boy, Jackson, sometimes pulls them out and puts them in his room. These old, dusty, falling apart trophies bring back fond memories.

In grade school, I was always an average student. I actually hated school, but on the other hand, I never had any real problems with the schoolwork itself, making decent grades. I remained shy throughout my school years and never looked forward to going. I went to school in the grunge era, when everyone wanted to look like Kurt Cobain, and I was sporting a neat and tidy, parted hairdo while everyone called me the "Karate Kid." I was pretty lonely in high school, and so, for me, those years were a matter of just trying to "get by." My focus was karate. With a small five-foot-eight frame, I weighed 128 pounds soaking wet when I finished high school, so I didn't play sports like football or basketball. Karate was what I was really skilled at, and so it became such an important part of my life it took up most of my free time. It was at the karate school that I felt like I belonged and fit in.

When I look back through the photo albums, belt certificates, and trophies that I won, I really miss those days. I ask myself, "What lessons did I learn in those years?" There's a ton of them, but one thing that I am so thankful for is my family. I know that the solid structure I had at home was the backbone of my early childhood success.

KNOCKOUT NUGGETS

1. *Confidence is like a muscle.* The more you develop it and work on it, the more confidence you get. Trust me—you can never have too much confidence. Don't confuse confidence with arrogance; there's a big difference between the two! I've learned to speak in public, negotiate business deals, and do things I don't think many people thought I could achieve. If you are going to build a big business, you have to build your confidence so you can handle the tough stuff. With encouraging parents and a big brother to look up to, I was encouraged to always try my best even when I was the smallest in the class. The guiding principle I grew up with was "Hudsons never quit!" At least that's what my dad always said. The motto around my house was, if you start something, see it all the way through.

    And how you dress affects how confident you feel. My karate uniform was important to me; when I put it on, I felt like I was part of something that mattered. Since you are the CEO of your life, let's get you in the CEO mind-set. This mind-set is three pronged. First, you must put on your *CEO outfit.* When I slip on my best shoes, my nicest watch, my 9Round logoed shirt, and my dry-cleaned creased pants, I feel like I could conquer the world. Now most days around the office you will see me in 9Round workout clothes, but when I have potential franchisees coming in, I always dress to impress. I want people to see that I care about every detail. The second thing you must do is a physical movement of some sort. I call it a *power move*! Personally, I look in the mirror, throw a few punches (shadowboxing), and look straight into my hazel eyeballs. The third component is a *power statement*. I take a deep breath and deliver mine: "I'm a magical machine of success." What's *your* CEO outfit? What's *your* power move? What's *your* power statement? Why don't you take a few minutes and write it right here on this page.

I'm serious. _____

2. *Embrace the thrill.* Testing for belts in karate, stepping in the ring, selling a membership, awarding a franchise, improving and building a specific area in my business— these are all things that keep the fire going in my belly. These are the things that get me excited on a Sunday night. Of course I am nervous, but those nerves keep you on your toes and mentally alert. They are there for a reason. My boxing coach always taught me that if you're nervous, that's a good thing—it means you have enough passion to really care. He would say, "If you're not nervous, then I'm really nervous." I will share more about him later in this book.

CHAPTER TWO

FAMILY

A lot of success stories have chapters about how dysfunctional and chaotic their own childhoods were. I hate to disappoint you, but that was *not* my case. I was raised in small-town South Carolina with only one brother. We were a tight family of four and about as middle class as you could get. We didn't live in a mansion but had a nice, three-bedroom home in a good neighborhood with a swimming pool. We didn't have everything, but we never lacked for anything either. Of course, my parents spoiled me and my big brother—at least that's what they said. Those days were so simple it seemed.

We were a small family living in a small town just like an Andy Griffith episode. (By the way, *The Andy Griffith Show* is still one of my favorite shows.) I remember riding my bike as a kid without a helmet (nobody wore helmets in those days) around the neighborhood with my close friends. Mom and Dad's rule was, "Be home by dark." Today, most parents wouldn't let their kid walk to the neighbor's house by themselves. My parents have been married almost fifty years as I write this—an amazing feat with today's high divorce rates. Because of my small family and simple upbringing, I consider family to be one of life's greatest blessings. I have my parents to thank for that. They are hardworking people from small-town America who instilled in me the values, drive, and ambition to achieve extraordinary things. To understand me, you have to understand my parents.

My father, Ray Hudson, was the youngest of nine. He was born in 1945 on a farm in the tiny agricultural upstate community of Greer, South Carolina. The nearest "big cities" were Greenville and Spartanburg. Being a farm family with nine kids, my dad's family never had much, and on top of that, my dad's father died of a heart attack at the young age of fifty-five when Dad was only sixteen. As I heard it, this news was very hard for my dad to take. My great-aunt Grace, who is ninety-five years old at the time I'm writing this, recalls that she had never seen a sadder little boy than my dad when his father died. Everyone who ever knew John Esau Hudson always said that he was such a good man. I wish I could have known him.

My father went into the army, and when he returned from the service, in 1966, he married my mother, June. Unlike Dad, Mom was from a small family and has only one sister.

My parents were deeply devoted to their growing family, and they provided the kind of stable home environment that was ideal for raising kids.

Our family was about as average middle class as you could get. However, Dad was an entrepreneur at heart. I believe since he learned early how to run a farm and help care for his family after his father's passing, being a leader is naturally in his blood. After many jobs—such as a security guard, a pipe fitter, and a welder—he went into the business of buying and selling industrial equipment, such as valves and pipes. Mom worked as the secretary, helped run the office, and kept the books for the business. Given that we grew up around this environment, maybe it was inevitable that my brother and I would become enterprising self-starters too. We saw all the hard work that our parents did, everything from loading trucks to managing the sales cycle. Nobody really ever mentioned a "job" around my house. Rather, my parents instilled in us a mind-set, its guiding principle simple yet profound: find something that you enjoy, work hard at it, and provide for the family as best as you can.

I have much to be thankful for when it comes to how I was raised, but I realize that not everyone has this wonderful beginning. And there are many stories about how people rose up from really dysfunctional families to become positive leaders. They break the cycle. And the reverse is also true; people with great parents can do awful things. So remember—your past doesn't define you. You define you.

When I think back on how I was raised, I realize that I owe my parents so much; I am so grateful to them for my work ethic and dogged belief in American independence and individualism. Today's culture, steeped in an "entitlement attitude" is the exact opposite of how I think and live. So many people today, especially among the younger crowd, just don't know how to work their way up starting from the bottom. I see it in the college graduates who apply at our company for work. They expect to start with a six-figure salary and a secretary. *And they're not kidding!*

As a teenager finishing high school, I thought my parents didn't know anything. But now I realize how smart they were and still are. I guess that's part of growing up, right? Now I get it. The importance of being grateful for what you have and of having a very hard work ethic and a positive attitude are some of the things I learned as a kid growing up in the family business. I learned from Mom and Dad that if you want something badly enough, you can and should go and get it. It's not going to be given to you. Here's a quick bullet list of things that my mom and dad taught me (by action, not with lectures):

- Always tell the truth.
- Always work until the job is done. (Don't be a clock-watcher.)
- Do it right the first time.
- Pay close attention.
- *Listen!* There is a big difference between listening and hearing. Most people hear what others are saying but are not listening.

KNOCKOUT NUGGETS

1. *Family comes first.* Yes, family is a blessing. Today, my father is the only one out of nine kids who is still alive. He has seen his brothers and sisters all pass away. I bet he wishes he could speak to them all one more time. Whether you get along with your family or not, at least try to make amends. Try your best to have the best relationship you can with your family. You will never regret trying.

2. *Your past does not have to lead to your future.* Understand that it doesn't matter what your upbringing was. Not all successful people had dysfunctional families and lived in the ghetto. Understand that I am not the classic example of the impoverished person pulling him or herself up by the bootstraps. Neither

am I a person who was born into an empire of wealth. I come from a middle-class family with a solid basis in work ethics and togetherness. Successful people come from all walks of life. Leaders are made and developed, not born. I hope you underlined that sentence and put a star beside it! Leaders are not born; they are *made.* Starting your own business is the best leadership-making machine there is. It will force you to grow in every way possible. It will test your inner discipline and perseverance, and *if* you decide to take on being an entrepreneur, you will develop skills that will *never* leave you. Once you develop these magical, sought after leadership skills, you will be a different person—a better person, a powerful person. When you walk into a room, you will hear people whisper, "There he or she is."

3. *You ain't entitled to anything.* Yep, you heard me. Quit thinking that the government, your parents, the weather, the economy, or anything or anyone for that matter is why you are where you are. One thing I can assure you: *you are exactly where you are in life because of what went into your mind and what actions you have taken.* Once you swallow that pill, then you can move on and do something about it. A couple of my top club owners in the 9Round system, a husband-and-wife team, told me when they signed the franchise agreement with 9Round that they only had $118 in their checking account. These folks took full responsibility for themselves and made things happen. They have a beautiful family of three children. One child has special needs, so you can only imagine how busy they are. However, they have three very successful 9Round locations, often landing in our

top grossing clubs over and over each month. That's the beauty of living in America. It doesn't matter what has happened to you in the past or where you start your journey. You can succeed if you realize one thing: success is a ladder you climb, not a bed you lie in.

CHAPTER THREE

OPPORTUNITY KNOCKS

As I neared the end of high school, I was pretty sure what I was going to do for a career. I decided to go into elementary education and become a teacher. It seemed like a natural fit; I had always so enjoyed teaching martial arts to kids.

My plans to make a career out of teaching seemed to be off to a good start. I was accepted at the University of South Carolina and attended classes at the campus in Spartanburg (today called USC Upstate) beginning in 1997. Located in the foothills of the Blue Ridge Mountains, the campus was only a twenty-five-minute drive from where I lived, so I commuted rather than living at school. Maybe I missed out on some of the fun of campus life, but then again, not having to pay for room and board made going to school much less expensive, and it allowed me to continue working in the karate school even as a college student.

I didn't love college, but it was so much less confining than high school had been. In addition to working as a karate teacher for my brother at the karate school he bought (more on that in a later chapter), I could also work out between classes; the ability to fit regular exercise into my routine is something that's always been vitally important to me. I've never wanted to let my training lapse. Also, even though I was still living at home, for the first time, I felt a real sense of independence. Those were good years, and I look back on them with a smile. However, as one year progressed into the next, I began to question my future. Was teaching elementary school what I really wanted to do with my life?

It's true that I had always wanted to lead and to teach. In fact, I had been working for Kevin ever since I was thirteen. At first, he gave me small teaching jobs—nothing major. But as I grew and got better at it, he gave me more to do. By the age of sixteen or seventeen, I was teaching full martial arts classes to both kids and adults.

I have fond memories of those days. The classes were great, and I loved going through the drills with my students. I learned some valuable skills in those days that, at the time, I didn't realize I was learning. It's crazy how life sometimes works that way. Life can be a natural teacher if we just pay attention. Here are three important things that I realize as I reflect back have paid off big-time for me.

- I learned how to teach and lead. Being able to get a three-year-old or a fifty-year-old to do things he or she normally doesn't do is quite an accomplishment. I learned how to instruct and work with people of all ages and from all walks of life. Today, this helps me so much, as I have many different franchise owners and personalities to deal with.

- I learned valuable communication skills. I became better at being able to get my point across in an encouraging way instead of a forceful way. Think about it; I can ask a kid to come over here in two ways.
  A) I can say, "Johnny, I want to see how fast you can run to me. Ready, set, *go!*
  B) I can physically pick Johnny up while he is kicking and screaming while saying to him, "You had better get over here!"

  Both will get the job done, but scenario A will be much more encouraging and pleasant for both of us.

- I also learned patience and enthusiasm. As they say, "Patience is a virtue." Two of the most important qualities of any teacher are patience and enthusiasm. Here's one of my favorite sayings, "Enthusiasm isn't taught, it's caught." Think back to one of your favorite teachers in middle school or high school. I bet they had both of these qualities. In fact, one of our foundational principles in the 9Round franchise is what we call *E Squared*. This stands for *energy and enthusiasm!* We make sure that everyone who comes into our system is full of E Squared.

Even though I knew teaching kids was very satisfying for me, as the end of college neared, I started to seriously question whether life as a teacher (in the public schools at least) was right for me. I was in my senior year and even to the point of student teaching when these doubts surfaced. I found the red tape that teachers are put through was discouraging my creativity and joy in the teaching field. On top of that, what teachers earn in a salary in no way reflects the importance of their role of shaping our children. Yes, I was well aware of the career path that I, and my parents, had assumed I would take. At the time, they were very keen on the idea of college as the ideal means of getting a good job and enjoying a better life. Quitting wasn't an option, and I needed to make my college education a success.

But then I had a defining moment in my life that I will never forget. I read a book called *Rich Dad Poor Dad* by Robert Kiyosaki. That book broadened my horizons about how important it is for me to increase my financial intelligence and my views about money. It tells the story of the author, who grew up being influenced by two dads, his own and his best friend's dad. The author's own father had been a school superintendent. He was a very smart, well-educated guy, but he lived paycheck to paycheck and could never seem to get ahead. His friend's dad owned many businesses and was wealthy—and didn't have even a high school education. It opened my eyes to the fact that financial security is not 100 percent based on a formal education or degrees that you earn. I was so inspired that I quickly forgot about becoming a teacher for $28,000 per year.

It was during my senior year in college that I went on journey of self-discovery, self-learning. I poured myself into self-help motivational books, and you could always find me listening to tapes about entrepreneurial topics, such as sales, marketing, or wealth-building strategies. They were all preaching the same thing; you need to work harder on yourself than on your job—a concept I was (and still am) in agreement with 100 percent.

With all these ideas percolating in my head, during my last year of college, I made a key decision and enrolled in a number of business and communications courses. It was time to explore a new direction.

BECOMING A BUSINESS OWNER

Simultaneously, my brother gave me a golden opportunity when he suggested that I could partner with him in his karate school. Twelve years prior to this, when Kevin was eighteen, he had purchased the school that we had both trained in since we were young kids. The owner had been behind on rent at the time and having trouble making a go of it, so he offered it to one of his best, my brother. My dad had loaned Kevin the money, and Kevin had taken over.

This new idea of being a business owner excited me. Things were happening rapidly, and my head was spinning. However, my parents were getting a little fed up. If I was to partner with my brother while still finishing school, I would have to cut my schooling back to part-time, and that meant it would be another two years before I would to graduate. My parents took a stand. They wanted me to hurry up and graduate. I don't blame them at all.

When it was all said and done, I partnered with my brother, and I graduated with a bachelor's of science degree called interdisciplinary studies in May 2003. Thank God I was finally finished. And thank God my GPA was not printed on the diploma.

For years, I was a very important part of the school Kevin ran and put in a lot of sweat equity, but still it was an extraordinary act of generosity when he gifted me a 25 percent share of the business. As I said, it was the place where both of us had trained as kids, so it felt like a second home to us. The name Greer/Lyman School of Karate just didn't have the same zing as Hurricane Martial Arts Center, so it was exciting when

Kevin could name a karate school that referenced the name he used in competitive kickboxing, Kevin "Hurricane" Hudson.

This was when I officially became a business owner. This was when things changed for me, and it was really exciting. I was finishing up college and owned part of a business that I loved very much and had an incredible amount of passion about. I was growing up and learning to become an entrepreneur. It was an exciting time, and my brother and I were "rock stars" in our little community.

IN THE RING

Along with learning about business and my direction in life, competitive kickboxing was a huge part of my life, and the same was true for my brother. My big brother actually won two world titles. What an accomplishment! Combat sports were perfect for me because I was naturally very fast and had extremely good coordination.

During my college years, I did actually bulk up when I found a love for weight lifting. I was tired of being a small-framed kid, and I wanted to put on more muscle. I started lifting almost every day, and on top of that, I remember packing seven or eight peanut butter sandwiches in my bag daily. And the goal each day was to eat all of them. The plan worked. In a couple of years, I was up to 175 pounds and was strong as an ox—strong and fast, a deadly combination.

However, I learned that the heavier you are, the taller the opponents seem to get. I'll never forget fighting a tree one day by the name of Kevin "the Hit Man" Engle in Cedar Rapids, Iowa, at the IKF National Amateur Tournament (one of the biggest amateur kickboxing tournaments in the world). Engle was six foot two and why he had the fight name "the Hit Man" was no mystery. Remember—this guy probably walked around at 185 or 190 pounds, dropping weight just for the fight, as is common in the combat sports world. When he stepped up to the ring, I looked at my corner man (my brother) and said, "Is that guy really in my weight class?"

This guy could not have hit harder. Every opponent prior to me ended up on the floor, knocked out cold. Everyone was sure I was next. I'll tell you, the Hit Man had a right hand that hit like a truck. It was toe-to-toe for three rounds. But I was slick and fast. He didn't knock me out or even knock me down, but he did still win the fight. It was after that that I rethought my weight class and made the decision to drop back into a lighter division. I lessened up a little on my weight training, and I found my most comfortable zone was right around 147 to 154 pounds. That's the welter to light middleweight division. This meant I could walk around at about 165 pounds between fights and just lose a little right before a competition without much difficulty. That made me a really strong light middleweight fighter.

Sparring in a karate classroom on a mat is one thing, but when you step through those ropes into a real fighting ring, there's no holding back! You can hit as hard as you want. That's quite different from the formal karate tournaments, where you can't just go wild and hit as hard as you want or you will be disqualified. I liked being able to go full force in the ring!

Combat sports are not for the weak at heart. During my career, I suffered a broken hand and a broken nose, not to mention hundreds of bruises, knots, and cuts. I look back on those days, and I'm actually proud of those wounds. I remember every punch in battle. Maybe I'm a little weird, but hey, who isn't?

Some of the best times in my young adulthood included amateur kickboxing. Some bouts were held in school gyms or in armories. But a lot of the shows would be on a combined pro and amateur venue in bars and nightclubs. Often those were in some pretty rough areas. You never knew exactly what you'd see. I can remember once going to fight in a brewery in Atlanta. Obviously, they were selling beer, lots of it. By the time I walked from the dressing rooms to the ring, my brother had to wipe my bare feet off because I'd waded through so much beer. But, whether it was in a high school gymnasium or a rowdy bar, every show was well attended, and the energy the crowds brought was infectious.

The mental pull for me with kickboxing was that each fight was its own short-term goal. You're working toward it. It was just like karate, where you have belts to reach for. I would have maybe twelve weeks or so to work up to each event. I grew up thriving on that short-term goal mentality. There was just always something you had to think about every day to reach your goal—something to work toward.

As the years went on, the wins piled up! I won numerous amateur titles in boxing and kickboxing, including the following:

- North Carolina Golden Glove boxing champion
- Regional FX Toughman
- Southeastern FX Toughman
- IKF (International Kickboxing Federation) East Coast Amateur Kickboxing title
- IKF North American Amateur Kickboxing title
- WKKO United States Kickboxing title (this organization doesn't exist anymore)
- WKA (World Kickboxing Association) United States Kickboxing title

While most fights were just single, one-on-one matches, occasionally I fought in bracket style tournaments, similar to playoffs. In these, there might be fifteen fighters in your division, and if you win, you go to the next bracket. As a competitor, you might fight four or five times at a single tournament, which certainly gives you a lot of experience, and you can really build your record up quickly.

I was honored to be on the US Kickboxing Team in Switzerland for the IAKSA (today known as WAKO) in an international kickboxing event. I stepped into the giant auditorium that was housing the event and, for a moment, silently took everything in. It was the largest amount of people I'd ever seen at one competition. It was very similar to the Olympics. The excitement was intense! There were four rings of fights going all at once, with competitors from all over the world. In this upcoming four-day tournament, I would fight one or possibly two fights every day. I had trained hard for this, and I was mentally ready.

My first fight was against a German guy, and I won. So far, so good. We had been there since 9:00 a.m., and it was already 9:00 p.m., so my team and I left the building, assuming we were finished for the day. Thirty minutes later, we got phone calls asking where the heck we were! I had another fight that night, and it had to be done right away! We had no idea how communications got crossed, and we tried to book it back to the venue. But we weren't quick enough. I got disqualified. Talk about frustrating! I'd come all the way across the world for this, and I barely got to compete. That's the world of kickboxing for you. It's exciting, but the coaches are not always the most organized.

It was hard to enjoy sightseeing over the next four days until our flight home. Switzerland was a beautiful country though. At least I got to see it.

That was the high point of my amateur career. In 2005, I made the decision to turn pro so that I could accept the incredible opportunity to fight on the WCL (World Combat League). This new team fight league was invented by the legendary martial artist and movie star Chuck Norris. I didn't hesitate for one second to fight on his league. Talk about decisive.

It was so much fun, and the event was really well organized and felt very "Hollywood." We had team uniforms, and between interviews with the press and flashing cameras, there was plenty of PR hoopla. The matches were even broadcast on the Versus channel. That first event went really well. The fighter caliber was elite, so in the event, I won the first half, and my opponent won the second half. I was still pleased. Considering that I was in Dallas, fighting a guy *from* Dallas, I couldn't help but be very pleased with the outcome.

No matter how fancy the league, professional kickboxing doesn't pay a lot of money. But Chuck Norris's league was more than a step above fighting in bars, so I happily stayed with it for three seasons.

I fought at some great venues, including the Mohegan Sun casino in Connecticut, as well as San Antonio, Las Vegas, and many other popular venues.

Fast-forward a few years to the later part of my professional kickboxing career, I traveled to Canada and fought an opponent named Muzamall Nawaz in his hometown of Toronto (he was from Burlington, a Toronto suburb).

The trip was especially hard on me. I had traveled all day and was required to go straight to a doctor's office to get a CT scan. This is a required protocol for the Canadian Athletic Commission. I was so tired, I was dozing off in the CT scan machine. Then, I went straight to weigh-ins.

The fight itself went ten grueling rounds, and I lost the decision. It was really close, and I felt that I just didn't do enough to win. Of course, in someone else's hometown, it's pretty much of an unwritten rule that if you're going to win, you're going to have to win by a knockout. That's just kickboxing politics.

But it wasn't over. About a year later, Nawaz offered me a rematch, this time for the IKF (International Kickboxing Federation) World Title. This was what I had waited for my entire life—*a world title fight!* I jumped at the opportunity and immediately started training for the bout that was to take place on October 1, 2011.

It was scheduled for twelve rounds. The fight was held in the London Convention Center in London, Ontario, and it was an awesome occasion, a classy black-tie event with a charity auction. I was thinking, *This will be a nice place to win the world title.* It certainly was a lot better than a bar!

I flew my wife up to sit ringside. She was sitting in the audience, surrounded, for the most part, by Nawaz fans. She barely ate a bite at dinner she was so nervous for me, but in a good way. She's never been nervous that I'll get hurt. Rather, in her words, "It's like every punch Shannon throws is my punch. Every kick is my kick with him. Mentally, it's nerve-racking to watch him fight because I just want him to win." I later found out that in the ladies room before the fight began, my wife struck up a conversation with a woman who told her she was in a room full of Nawaz fans.

My wife, without even thinking, and with a twinkle in her eye, quickly said, "I'm sorry, but he's going to lose."

She was right. The fight went really well. The first few rounds were slightly even, but I was doing just enough to show that I was dominating. But remember the rule? When you're fighting in the opponent's hometown, you better knock him out if you want the win. In the sixth round, I hit him with a right hook and knocked him down. He got up, and I kicked him in the head with a roundhouse kick and knocked him down again in that same round. He got up right as the bell sounded, ending round six. When the bell rang for round seven, he did not come out. At first I didn't realize what was happening, but when I saw the ref waving his hands overhead in the air, I knew he had stopped the fight. That meant the victory was mine. The next thing I remember was standing on the ropes, my hands in the air. I have no idea how my wife got up in the ring as fast as she did, but she ran in her heels all the way there. It was a TKO. I was *the* World Champion.

My adrenaline was so high that it was a few minutes before I realized how tired I was. I whispered to my wife as she was hugging me, "I think I'm going to puke." I received $2,400 for that fight. I have a longstanding joke that after I paid my wife's way up and she bought a new dress and got her hair done, I didn't make anything! Obviously, this was never about the money, it was about pride and accomplishment. That night was one of the very best moments in my life.

As an interesting side note, I actually made much more money in the WCL (Chuck Norris's league). There was even bonus money if your team won. If you knocked out your opponent, you got more. It's a nice way to play the sport. You get more reward the better you perform. Pro boxing matches aren't that way. You get paid the same—win or lose. I'm a huge fan of performance-based rewards myself.

I do remember this one fight when I got my butt really handed to me on the WCL. The silver lining came when I was walking back to the dressing room and heard my name called. It was none other than Chuck Norris himself, who was with his entourage. The famous star gave me a big hug and said, "Good fight."

I was thinking, *Really?!* He always picked "fight of the night," and that night it was mine. My opponent and I had both done a skillful job showing the art of kickboxing, and Chuck really appreciated that. He gave each of us a five hundred-dollar bonus. It was a great moment that I will never forget.

I can see how well kickboxing fit with my personality. It didn't further my life economically, but it taught me how to set and reach goals, how to make adjustments needed for success, not to give up, and how to break down big goals into smaller steps. Sometimes the dreams we have are starting points for what we need to develop within ourselves so that we can move on. And the beautiful thing is that we all have these life lessons, whether it's a job, a career, a project at school, or a relationship. Mine was kickboxing, but yours is something else. Each dream has a seed that grows into an experience, and sometimes those experiences give us what we need to go forward into other areas, and the economic rewards follow later. I learned a lot when I was in college, but I learned just as much through these experiences, even though I didn't earn much money.

Today at thirty-five, I'm semiretired from professional kickboxing. Will I ever step into the ring again as a pro? Stay tuned.

KNOCKOUT NUGGETS

1. *Turn off the TV and read a book.* The average household has the TV on seven hours a day. One of the great things that my wife and I have in common is that we are always reading something to make us grow. *Rich Dad Poor Dad* really got me motivated at a young age, and from then on I started learning about other books that chronicled people's paths to success. I realized, wow, all the information is out there somewhere; all I have to do

is study and *learn from it.* Today, I still enjoy reading a good book. Often, my favorite types of books are about someone who founded a brand, among them Ray Kroc, Dave Thomas, Henry Ford, or Sam Walton. Another one of my all-time favorite writers and speakers Jim Rohn said, "Poor people have big TVs, and rich people have big libraries." (I personally believe you can have both.) I hear people say, "I don't have time to read." Well, you have to make time. Also, create a habit of reading. I always try to read just a few pages while lying in the bed before I go to sleep. When you squeeze in a few pages here and there (in the bathroom even), you would be surprised how fast you can get through a book.

Here's a good list of recommended reading so you can start your own personal library:

- *Think and Grow Rich* by Napoleon Hill
- *Rich Dad Poor Dad* by Robert Kiyosaki
- *The Richest Man in Babylon* by George S. Clason
- *The Compound Effect* by Darren Hardy
- *The Art of Persuasion* by Bob Burg
- *The Secret* by Rhonda Byrne
- *The Power* by Rhonda Byrne
- *The Science of Being Great* by Wallace D. Wattles
- *The Game of Life and How to Play It* by Florence Scovel Shinn
- the Bible

2. *It is not always about the money.* Live your passion for the life experience. Even though I only got paid $2,400 for my world title fight, I didn't care. The title was what I really wanted. I soaked up every minute of that

experience—from the training sessions and sparring to eating right and getting oxygen treatments to heal and repair faster. The point here is that sometimes you should do things for the experience and what it does for your mind, not just for your bank account. Experiences and dreams followed are priceless.

3. *Sometimes it's all about the money.* One of the reasons I changed my major from early childhood development to business was the unfortunate fact that teachers just don't get paid what they're worth. I had a bigger vision, and it's important to recognize when to draw the line and not sell yourself short. I think I've had this inner knowing since I was very young because of something that happened one Sunday at the Methodist Church I grew up attending. During each service, the pastor's wife would bring the children up for a minilesson about the Bible, and the parents would watch. This particular day, the pastor's wife asked all us kids, "Does anyone know what a prophet is?"

I quickly raised my hand and said, "It's the money you have left over after you pay all the bills."

I remember the entire congregation burst out in laughter. It was that moment that my parents knew I would be a business guy. This is my wife's favorite story.

CHAPTER FOUR

EXPANSION

As you can see, martial arts and kickboxing are passions of mine. Just a couple of years after owning a karate school with my brother and as I traveled for kickboxing, I was thinking about how I could make this work for me as my life's work. I thought about the possibility of forming a martial arts chain, though Kevin and I had no specific ideas about expanding at first.

However, in many ways Kevin and I are polar opposites. He's more laid-back than I am and very conservative. I'm the opposite. I'm bouncing off the walls with energy and ideas and like to implement new ideas quickly—so quickly that I often take the "ready, fire, aim," approach. This contrast made for a good team because each of us was able to bring to the table a quality the other did not have. We balanced each other out. But along with differences come disagreements and arguments. Sometimes we didn't get along at all, though I guess that's pretty typical for brothers.

For many business owners, expansion is a natural inclination. Kevin was a bit reluctant, but I convinced him that it would be in our best interests to open a second location. After all, we had seen other martial arts schools owners do it successfully. Why couldn't we? We were both involved with the expansion, but I was the primary driving force behind it. This was in 2005. We found a suitable spot about eight miles away in the small town of Taylors, South Carolina.

The new school quickly became a big success. The full-time manager we brought on, Steve Foy, was a part owner. We gave him a 49 percent interest in the school, and he also put up some of his own money to build the location out. Steven was a black belt, a ranking he had earned at our original school. Hiring from within is something I continue to be a fan of to this day. During the years Foy spent earning his black belt with us, he'd been working in a machine shop and hated it, so he was extremely enthusiastic about the idea when we offered the managing position to him. We did several things right with that business decision.

1. We found someone who had a passion for martial arts and was ready for a change. You can't teach passion.
2. We required him to put up some of his own money, so he had "skin in the game." This helped motivate him to make the business a success.
3. We hired from within. We knew him, and he knew us, so the trust factor was there.
4. We trained with him weekly. I remember sitting in the karate school after a workout reviewing our sales scripts. We called it "scriptinese."

We employed a lot of marketing strategies, including grassroots marketing, introductory specials, on-the-street marketing, and direct mail. Of course, we also had a grand opening, which brought in a good flow of students. One thing my brother and I always had along with well-developed martial arts skills and teaching ability was that we made it our business to be very savvy in marketing and selling.

One of the strategies we employed that still works well today is a low-cost introductory offer of some sort. When you have a great service, no matter what it is, the key is to get as many people as possible to give it a test drive, so to speak. This works well for any service-based business. We would constantly run promos such as "thirty days *free*" or "two introductory lessons plus a uniform for only $19.95." As I mentioned earlier, I was engrossed in many business marketing and sales books and also networked and studied with other martial art business owners, but I was largely self-taught. I was also very quick to apply what I had learned.

If there's one skill you have to master in any business, it's selling. Selling often has a bad reputation, but it's mostly communicating to influence prospective clients without alienating people. Here are a couple of selling basics I have learned:

1. Strike while the iron is hot. It's important to ask for the sale during the very first visit. If you wait, life might happen, and the prospect might not come back. Also, people are the most excited at the beginning of any relationship. Remember—people buy with emotion and then justify with logic. Get prospects excited and emotional, and then ask for the sale.

2. Give choices and ask open-ended questions. I learned early that it's how you ask that is the trick. Instead of saying, "Do you want to sign up?" we would say, "Which program works best for you, our basic program or our leadership program?" We still teach these same techniques in our 9Round Franchise Training program today.

Let me tell you—the skill of selling is one you can apply to many aspects of your life. Believe me, I am always selling every day in every way. I have to sell my kid on going to bed, I have to sell my wife on eating at my favorite restaurant, and of course I have to sell my staff on my vision of making 9Round a worldwide brand. Once you learn how to sell, you will have confidence to market like crazy. No matter how good your product or service is, if you don't get people excited enough about it to give it a try, you will never make a sale.

My brother and I actually eagerly embraced this side of being business owners. I know that this is a major part of what made our schools so successful. Many skilled martial artists are out there teaching, but not all of them love the sales and marketing side of owning. They want to teach and share their knowledge, but they don't necessarily *enjoy* the groundwork that is required to gain the audience needed to make the teaching possible. If you can't sell, you won't have anyone to teach. So a good lesson here is that you need to learn how to market and sell, and there are many ways to do that, including reading, attending classes, finding mentors, visiting other businesses, and just learning from your mistakes.

The launch of our second school went quite smoothly, in large part because we already had a good reputation in the community. That made it much easier to get up and running.

It segued nicely from the original school, and of course, we were careful to keep each location as a separate entity for liability purposes. This new location also changed my life in another way.

WHEN IT'S RIGHT ...

It just so happened that, at the grand opening celebration, a beautiful girl named Heather drove up to inquire about self-defense and karate lessons for her and her daughter. She explained to my brother that she was going through a divorce and felt she needed to learn self-defense, seeing as she went home alone now. I know that cupid has many arrows, but when I saw that woman for the first time, I was instantly in love. I hadn't thought of dating someone with a child before, but I loved kids, and I didn't mind that Heather had a little girl. I figured her daughter would be as wonderful as her mother. The only snag was, I had a girlfriend of seven years! Family and friends had been asking for more than a while when we were getting married, and I was seriously considering that as my next step.

However, one night I was out with a buddy of mine, and we ran into this new girl. It was her twenty-seventh birthday, and she was out with her girlfriends. She saw me and came up to say hello. I remember her saying, "You probably don't recognize me in my regular clothes!" (In the karate world, we joked about how we always wore "pajamas" to work, meaning the karate uniforms. Everyone looked the same in those, so I knew exactly what she meant.) Without hesitation, I told her, "You look great either way!" She looked surprised at my obvious flirtatious attempt, but she also didn't look disappointed. Incidentally, my girlfriend was out of town that weekend, and my buddy and all Heather's friends ended up staying out until 4:00 a.m. that night! That was it for me. I was officially in love with Heather. I actually broke up with the girl I had been dating for seven years.

What a crazy time! My friends and especially my parents thought I was nuts and thought Heather was just trying to sabotage my relationship with my girlfriend. Heather was not officially divorced on paper, but her divorce was being finalized and there was a lot of red tape. Top that off with me breaking it off with a girl who everyone in my karate school knew and loved, and Heather quickly unofficially got the award for "Most Disliked New Student." She knew what people must have thought about her, and she tried hard not to let it bother her, but I knew better; Heather was really hurt.

While I knew that my friends thought they were just looking out for me, I knew in my heart what was true for me. Heather made me happy and complete. I was at a time in my life where I was ready to build a career and make some money. I needed someone to support that and help me focus. She was the one for me. I could talk to Heather about subjects that were very deep and personal to me, and it was exciting to have a partner who was so like-minded.

My point here is this: always trust your gut and inner voice. Some call it "a gut feeling"; others refer to "God" or "the Divine" or "the universe." Whatever you want to call it, *trust it!* Sometimes on the outside things don't look logical to your peers, but only *you* know if it's right.

The amazing thing about Heather was that she supported everything I did. She handled my crazy temper and harebrained ideas with such patience, love, and support. She was and still is an amazing support system in my life, and if it weren't for that support, 9Round might not exist today. To go against the grain and do what we did, with all the stress of family, friends, and not much money was quite a feat. Today, Heather is the co-founder of the 9Round Franchising LLC and has turned into an amazing businesswoman. She has also blessed me with two beautiful children—my beautiful stepdaughter, Elana, and my son, Jackson. It was an instant family for me. I like to joke and say, "Instant family, just add water!"

OUR THIRD LOCATION

While all those major life changes were happening, Kevin and I were simultaneously opening our third location. We knew another black belt who had also been one of our students and asked him if he would like to run location number three. He agreed, and we found a great location on the other side of town from our original school, in Greenville. The instructor's name was Kevin Ballenger. He'd been a student six years before this, but had laxed on his training. He was working a job he had no passion for and was actually having thoughts of a career change anyway. When we approached him, he had already started taking karate again, and he was getting back to his former fit and disciplined self. He had forgotten how much he loved martial arts and was on track with finding himself again. He got in shape very quickly and was highly motivated.

However, school number three wasn't an automatic success. It was a slow go. The location was farther away than our second school, and so this new school didn't benefit as much from our solid reputation as our other two schools did.

Perhaps even more significantly, Ballenger didn't have the business training he should have had. Looking back, I see that the fault lay with Kevin and me. We should have slowed down and given him a more solid business plan and more direction. This is a common mistake with people who try to grow too quickly. They get starry-eyed and throw a location up, stick someone in, and say, "Go!" They stop by once a week or so and then wonder why this new location isn't doing as well as the location they are working in every day.

We saw the problems mount within just a couple of months. One problem, besides Ballenger's lack of training, was that the rent was high and the overhead wouldn't be sustainable for long if member enrollments didn't pick up.

Financial stress can cause many problems. You've probably heard of marriages breaking up because of fights about money. That's why it's so important to not make decisions when emotions are high. I learned that lesson not just once but a few times. While the anxiety surrounding school number three was building, we had a current martial arts student go out and start his own karate school less than a mile and literally right around the corner from our headquarter school. This is very common in the martial arts world. Egos get really big, really fast. He tried to steal our students, and let me tell you, that did not sit well with us. Did I mention I have a temper that sometimes goes from zero to sixty in seconds? Of course, my brother wanted to just let it ride, which looking back, I realize really was the right way to address it. But this became the subject of another disagreement between Kevin and me. I stewed on the situation constantly and let it get under my skin more and more. I ended up taking a few actions that I regret. My brother was so upset with me that he didn't even want to teach with me in the same school anymore. He basically sent me to the struggling third location and told me to go and get that school right.

CHALLENGES

Feeling "banished" from my second home made for a challenging time emotionally and was probably the hardest thing I've ever dealt with. Our original karate school was a family business. My mother worked there as the secretary, and I'd see her every night. After work, my brother and I usually talked on his drive home for thirty to forty-five minutes just recapping the day's activities and talking shop. This was my life, and yet, it would be almost two years before my brother and I were on good terms again.

While I embraced the challenge of raising membership enrollments at the new school, I hit a low point emotionally in my life. I felt a void without my brother and actually struggled with depression. I was angry that we disagreed, but I was also very sad. Sometimes it felt like someone had died. I didn't find out until years later that, at one point, my wife was so concerned that she called a hotline for people struggling with depression just to be sure that she could recognize the signs of a condition that needed someone to step in and help. My wife cares very much, and she's good at knowing when things aren't right. She was the one person I confided in during these times.

So I went over to work side by side with our partner, Ballenger, to pull the struggling school up. It seemed like a great opportunity to be on my own and prove to my brother that I could be a successful businessman doing it, my way. I took it as a personal challenge. This was a chance for me to implement some methods that I hadn't been "allowed" to do, per se, when it was me and my brother making decisions. As the founder of the schools, he almost always had the final decision. Now that we weren't really talking, I could call the shots for a while. So my attitude became: "Watch what I can do!"

I went out on the sidewalk in front of our newest school in my karate uniform with a sign that said Come Kick with Us! and listed the phone number. It was summer in South Carolina, and our climate is two things—hot and sticky. Ballenger and I would hold the signs and wave at cars. One of us would clip the business phone to our black belts in case it rang, and if it did, we would answer the calls right out there by the street and go for the appointment. We went to school festivals and other community events to drum up business. Within thirty days we had gained some real traction, and soon the numbers for the third school were looking up.

I was enjoying spreading my wings and seeing my methodology working before my eyes. It excited me, and I wanted to try even more things. I didn't have any fears holding me back because I felt like the worst thing had already happened. That kind of gutsiness can almost make you feel invincible. My wife was behind my ideas 100 percent, and my mind was going a thousand miles a minute. It started to become clear to me that I needed, once more, to step outside of my comfort zone and try something new. The winds of change were blowing yet again.

KNOCKOUT NUGGETS

1. *Expand your business.* You might not want to start a chain, but human nature actually has an intense desire to constantly expand. Flowers naturally bloom, trees naturally grow, and people either learn and expand their skills, or they get complacent, which is really resisting their true nature. Usually this resistance is based out of fear. I hear people say, "If I had a million dollars, I would never work another day in my life." That's probably the reason God will never allow you to have a million dollars—because you would quit and no longer contribute anything to society. Retire? I will never retire. I will always expand myself and keep creating something.

2. *Trust your gut, even if it makes others uncomfortable.* Your gut, or your heart, is your inner voice. Some call it the Divine or God. Whatever you want to call it, you must trust it. When Heather and I were trying to start our family, a lot of people around us second-guessed our decision; rumors about her intentions circulated, and people were clearly passing judgment on both of us. But I still knew that we were perfect for each other. We had very little money and I was having visions of a fitness chain that would shake up the entire industry. It wasn't logic; it was intuition. I'm glad I listened.

3. *Embrace the silence and listen.* Sometimes you might suddenly find yourself alone. This can be very scary. However, when you feel you have nothing left to lose, you often ironically find the bravery to do things you were previously too afraid to try. This period of unwanted solitude can end up being the best thing that ever happened to you. And that's why they say, "When you hit rock bottom, you've got nowhere else to go but up." You're either all in, or you curl up in a corner and quit. I'm not a quitter, so you can guess what happened next. One of my favorite Bible verses is Revelation 3:16 (KJV): "So, because you are lukewarm—neither hot nor cold—I am about to spit you out of my mouth." To me, this means commit and go for it! Don't be lukewarm.

CHAPTER FIVE

HARD BUSINESS LESSONS

When I was a twenty-four year old, I had finished college, but like most college graduates, I didn't have a lot of money. However, I took great pride in always paying what few bills I had on time. I really loved keeping my credit good and being punctual with my payments. This was another lesson I have learned from watching my parents over the years. Unfortunately, one day, I noticed my personal bank account was in the negative. What a terrible feeling in my stomach. Here I was, a college graduate, a great athlete, and a very smart person, and my account was negative. I will never forget. I scraped up a few measly bucks and went to the bank. I told the teller to write my balance on the deposit receipt please. She wrote it on the yellow receipt and slid the paper to me without saying a word. It said $1.72. I said to myself, *I don't like this feeling, and I will* never *feel this way again.* From that moment forward, I made a personal goal to be a multimillionaire by the time I was thirty-five years old.

The goal drove me to look at different business ventures, in addition to the martial arts facilities Kevin and I operated. I didn't always succeed at them. Sometimes you have to take the failures with the success. And unless you try something new, you can't grow toward your purpose.

DISCOVERING AN INSIDER'S VIEW

At that time, wanting to put on some muscle mass, I fell in love with weight training. My brother's friend from college, Olly Pierce, was a former bodybuilder with a massive frame. His nickname was "the British Bulldog" because he was originally from England. This guy was freakishly strong at six foot two, with bulging muscles. In fact, he couldn't even wear jeans because there were none that would fit his thigh's circumference. This guy ran a small personal training studio, and he offered me a part-time job so I could make some extra money. The most exciting thing about the time I spent working at the Bulldog's training studio turned out to be the education I received; Olly taught me the proper techniques and body mechanics of weight training and how to become stronger. I was hungry for that knowledge and just soaked it up. He was an amazing teacher, and I am forever grateful for all the British Bulldog taught me about weight training, stretching, and nutrition.

Not only did I learn a ton about health and nutrition, I got to observe firsthand the pros and cons of the one-on-one personal training business model. That gave me some valuable insights into the fitness business and helped expand my knowledge of how it worked. Again, I was always learning and thinking and jotting ideas down, which I still do today.

The secret here for you to take away is that in order to use all the knowledge and experience you gain, it's important to become a great *assembler*. Today, the 9Round kickboxing fitness business model is a combination of small group/class training and personal training put together. I've done a pretty good job of blending martial arts and fitness together. I think the only other person who has even come close is Billy Blanks with Tae Bo.

SCHOOL OF HARD KNOCKS

I had been privately training an adult student with kickboxing lessons. As it turned out, he was attending a local college to get his massage therapy license. We agreed to work out a trade, meaning I would train him one-on-one, and he would give me one massage a week. What a great life, right?! As it turned out, he was an incredible therapist and still is to this day, and I liked to call him Mr. Therapist. Mr. Therapist definitely had a gift and decided to start his own practice. He was extremely successful and was booked up every week. I was lucky to get a spot. I saw his talent, and an idea immediately popped into my head.

I wanted to bring massage therapy to the masses in a membership format. After all, membership businesses were my bread and butter. I told him the idea, and he immediately jumped on it, "Let's do it!" he said. So there we went. We leased a retail space close to both of us so we could easily keep a close eye on it. (This was all happening when my brother and I were still working together, prior to the opening of that third martial arts school. I guess I'm one of those serial entrepreneurs.) Mr. Therapist kept his original practice, and I of course kept running the karate school, with my brother at the time. We both chipped in money and started the new venture with a fifty-fifty partnership. Since we both had other jobs, his wife ran the day-to-day bookkeeping and scheduling. It seemed like a great plan.

Things were going great until one day I noticed the bank

account was in the negative. I pulled the bank statements and started looking them over carefully. There were many checks made out to cash. Last time I checked, I didn't have any employees named cash. As it turned out, Mr. Therapist's wife was stealing money from the company. This led to many arguments and disagreements between Mr. Therapist, his wife, and me. The next thing I heard, he and his wife were getting a divorce; he was cheating on her, and who knows what else was going on. It was a mess. We ended up shutting down the business and defaulting on the lease. Mr. Therapist and I unfortunately haven't spoken since.

Boy, did I learn some valuable lessons with that venture, among them:

1. Know your industry/craft and *be there*! I was not a massage therapist, so I had to rely on others to be the experts in that field. The plan was that Mr. Therapist would be responsible for training and monitoring the quality of the other therapists, and I would be the brains behind the business side of the venture. This could have worked if I had realized how much more time I needed to be in the business and not simply build it and expect success. A good therapist isn't enough. Businesses fail all the time from this type of belief. A good concept or product isn't enough. You have to have an active ownership (be there) in any business if you want it to succeed. I honestly think you have to be somewhat of a "control freak" to own your own business. If you are not, you won't be there to see if things are going wrong.

2. Know the score *every day*. The only way to keep score in business is with money. It's easy to count. Check the

bank account daily. My second mistake was putting too much trust in the Mr. Therapist's family to keep the finances straight when I should have kept things close to my chest. How was I to know there would end up being marital problems between my other two partners? Stuff happens, but I wasn't prepared enough for that.

3. If you bring on a partner in your business venture, be sure you vet them and set crystal clear guidelines on the roles required to make the business a success and on who is responsible for each of them. Next, put those roles in writing in an operating agreement so it's set in stone. Many people who are friends and go into business together let this formality slide because it feels too serious, or they feel that it's just unnecessary. But really, this is the only way both parties know what they are responsible for. A good friend will know that and have no problem with it.

It's too bad the venture Mr. Therapist and I attempted didn't work; I do believe I was onto something. In fact, today, there are several massage therapy chains that beat me to the punch with a membership-based model. Massage Envy, Elements, and Hand and Stone are just a few that have been wildly successful.

MY REAL ESTATE EMPIRE

As I was looking to expand into my niche, I hadn't forgotten what I'd read in other success stories. In almost all of them, real estate was in the mix somewhere. After all, no one is making any more acres of land on the earth these days, right? McDonald's, Donald Trump, and Robert Kiyosaki (author of *Rich Dad Poor Dad*) all own massive amounts of real estate.

The more I read, the stronger my desire to learn about real estate, rental property, and how to have someone else pay the rent while I built a great asset became. It's a beautiful strategy.

So one night, I was up late and saw an infomercial about how to buy rental property with "no money down." That was attractive to me because, of course, I didn't have any money to put down. At that time, banks were very generous, lending up to 100 percent of the value of a house, sometimes even more. The rule was, if you could fog a mirror and had a decent credit score, you could get a loan. For example, if a house was valued or appraised at $60,000, a bank would lend me $65,000 to cover closing costs and put a little in my pocket. Pretty good deal, right? All I had to do was to get the home rented for enough money to cover the mortgage payment, taxes, and insurance. It sounded like a great strategy, so this was exactly what I did with my first rental house.

I walked away from the closing table with keys in my hand to my very first rental house and a few thousand dollars in my pocket. Next, I purchased a For Rent sign and put it in front of the house with my cell number on it. Now I was in the rental business. Exciting stuff. But unfortunately, I had no clue what I was getting myself into. I did not know the various aspects of residential real estate and the rental business segment before I entered it, and that meant I was going to learn the hard way. If I had taken the time to study and talk with others in this field, I may have avoided some of the mistakes I made.

I had some horrible experiences with rental houses because of my ready, fire, aim strategy. I quickly realized that fielding, finding, and attracting renters was not as easy as I'd thought it would be. One night, my brother called me at around nine thirty and said, "Your house is on the news!"

I thought, *Oh no!* Well, sure enough, a drug deal had gone bad, and shots were fired. There is nothing worse than seeing your house on the news with police cars and yellow crime scene tape everywhere. The next day, I went to see the property, and there were bullet holes everywhere. Thank God, no one got hurt. I realized right then that I was in over my head, and I was thinking, *What have I gotten myself into?*

It's still a struggle at times to keep this rental above water, but I manage, and I've learned a lot. What's the lesson here? I will refer back to the first rule in my list of requirements for ensuring a business venture is successful. Learn your craft. Today I know far more about rental property, property valuation, appraisals, and the like. I learned the hard way so you don't have to. If you decide that real estate interest you, here are a few things I have learned.

1. Banks always have the power. In other words, the borrower *can be* a slave to the lender.
2. Be sure you put enough money down on a property so that you don't owe more than it's worth.
3. The money is really made when you buy, not when you sell. Buy low, sell high.

CAR WASH: ONE MORE PUNCH IN THE GUT!

There's one more business failure that I just have to share with you. Looking through the paper one day, I noticed that a local self-serve car wash was for sale. It was close to where I lived, and my brother and I considered going in together on it. The deal would be in the form of a combo loan that included the land as well as the business, so we figured that getting the car wash to pay for the land would be a great strategy. We went for it, and we were very excited. The only problem was, we didn't know anything about the car wash business.

I thought, how hard could it be? I'll just keep everything working and clean, and we should have a winner. If only it were that easy. Hoses would break, bays would get clogged up, the bill change machine would get jammed, vacuums would stop working, and the list goes on and on. What a headache! On top of that, I am not very mechanical or handy. I'm lucky to hammer a nail in straight. Just changing a hose posed a challenge for me.

One particularly fun story took place when I was doing one of my usual drive-by checks on the place. That night, I saw a man in the shadows without a car. He was acting shady and clearly not washing anything, so I pulled in to see what he was up to. I thought immediately that he was fiddling with the money holder, trying to steal something. I was very wrong. As I rounded the corner of one of the wash bays, he was pulling his pants up. He had just finished doing number two. I shit you not. Pun intended. It was the highlight of my career as a car wash owner.

On top of that, Kevin and I were only a few weeks in as owners when we discovered that the business pulled in about half what the previous owners had told us it did. Since it was a cash business, there was really no way to know exactly how much it brought in. The previous owners had five car washes, and the numbers for all five were lumped together on the profit and loss statements. Looking back, I realize that we should have looked at bank statements, but with the five operations combined, it was hard to tell which locations were doing what.

Now, you probably can tell how this story ends, right? *Foreclosure!* This happens when you can't make the payments on the property so the bank takes the property back. Now, my brother and I didn't hide from anyone; we face problems head on. We tried negotiating with the bank on a weekly basis, asking for more time. We requested an interest-only loan and then a deed in lieu of foreclosure—we tried anything and everything to prevent our losing the property.

Our attempts worked for a while, but eventually the bank took the property back and sold it at auction—and not even for the amount we owed on it. So my brother and I got slapped with what's called a "deficiency judgment." That hurt, and for the first time in my life, I couldn't pay the bills. This was one of the most humbling lessons I have ever learned. Also, I learned that there is a big difference between commercial property and residential property.

I knew that if I kept tinkering with these ideas and businesses, one day, I would find and create the perfect business for me. Even though I had a lot of disappointments, I kept fighting, and I knew in my gut that I had a great business in me somewhere. Please remember it only takes one good idea to make $1 million. Little did I know that my million-dollar idea was right around the corner.

KNOCKOUT NUGGETS

1. *Be careful with your credit.* A banker once told me there are only two things you need to do to be a success. These two things have stuck with me. The first is to always keep more money coming in than going out. The second is to always keep your credit good. Easier said than done, but these two lessons stick in my head each and every week.

2. *Action* is in the word *Attraction*. Isn't that interesting? As you can see from some of my business failures,

at least I took massive action. Think about it, in the caveman days, if you didn't get off your rear end and hunt for food, you went hungry. To be more attractive, take heavy action.

3. *Disgust is a powerful motivator!* The day I saw that negative bank balance, I decided to not to let that happen again. You may have a different motivator, but whatever it is, once you find it, creating a goal will be easier. Writing down my goals helps me to focus on them. A great exercise for you is to write your definite purpose in life.

I wrote my goal—my "definite purpose" in life in 2007, taking the wording from *Think and Grow Rich* by Napoleon Hill. I highly recommend this book if you haven't read it yet. I have the sheet of paper my goal is written on in my nightstand, and it's getting pretty ragged. I look at it often. Here is that goal word for word:

Shannon "The Cannon's" Definite Purpose

By January 1, 2015, I will have in my possession $1,000,000 cash, which will come to me in various amounts from time to time during the interim. In return for this money, I will give the most efficient service I am capable, rendering the fullest possible quantity, and the best possible quality of service in the capacity of owning multiple businesses, including martial arts/fitness, information marketing, real estate, etc.

I believe I will have this money in my possession. My faith is so strong that I can now see the money before my eyes. I can touch it with my hands. It is now awaiting transfer to me at the time and in the proportion that I deliver the service I intend to render for it. I am awaiting a plan by which to accumulate this money, and I will follow that plan when it is received.

I wrote this "definite purpose" before 9Round was in existence, very early in 2007. I had faith, and the idea of 9Round was given to me. I am a man of action. I took what was given to me and acted on it. What is your definite purpose? Write it now.

CHAPTER SIX

THE FLASH OF GENIUS

I had the karate school I was running and a new family to support. I was still pursuing a fighting career part-time. That's sort of an oxymoron because it's terribly difficult to pursue a fighting career only "part-time." Full time is really the way to go, but I was running a karate school and taking care of a new family meant full-time fighting wasn't a luxury I could afford. My passion for fighting had to be a part-time venture. The closest place I could get any type of legit sparring and training with other boxers was right outside of Atlanta in Decatur, Georgia. This was a two and a half hour-drive, one way. But I would make my way down and back in a day at least once a week, sometimes twice, especially if I was close to an upcoming fight. The legendary Xavier Biggs was my boxing trainer, and I'm still honored to have been able to fight under his coaching.

Mr. Biggs's gym was the real deal. Just walking into it was

quite an experience; it almost felt like stepping into a time warp. He had the real brick, autographed posters peeling off the walls, a huge roll-up garage door, jazz music playing, timers ringing, no AC, spit buckets, and a real boxing ring smack in the middle. Various hanging punching bags surrounded the ring. Most people have heard of a heavy bag or speed bag, but the double end ball, wrecking ball, and uppercut bag, to name just a few, might not be familiar to many. Each bag serves a different purpose for a fighter, allowing him or her to train for specific boxing moves and, therefore, working a different aspect of fighting.

Now, I would usually leave early from Greenville and get there midday so that I could spar and then leave to get back home by late afternoon to teach classes at the karate school. So I was often there to see a "lunch crowd." What I mean by that is—while I was up in the ring doing full-contact sparring, I would see executive businessmen come in, change out of their ties and nice shirts, and hit the bags, never stepping into the ring at all. Then they would change and go back to work. They were only there for a quick workout on the various bags. No contact. I was intrigued. This was the magical moment when I knew I could put some things together that could change the fitness industry.

THE IDEA EVOLVES

The long drive back home gave me plenty of time to think. I would think about what I should have done better in the ring and all the pointers Biggs had given me while I was there. I would also think about business.

When my brother and I ran the karate schools together, we offered a program called Kickbox Fitness. We held the class at eight o'clock at night, after the traditional karate classes were finished for the day, and we'd typically have a group of about ten to twenty at a time. I remember being physically and mentally exhausted after teaching high-energy kids' karate classes from three thirty in the afternoon all the way up until 8:00 p.m. But at eight o'clock, I would turn the music on, roll the mobile kickboxing bags out onto the mat, and start warming everyone up. It was kind of a relief to finally work with some adults at the end of the day, and I could be a little bit loose with my teaching style but still keep the class in line and give a brutal workout. Actually, that's what I became known for. When it came to providing a great workout, I always delivered. People would have a love-hate relationship with me. When they walked in the building, they knew it would be a tough workout, but they knew it was *exactly* what they needed. If Shannon "the Cannon" was instructing, you were gonna sweat.

At first, we offered the class two days a week. Then as enrollments picked up, we added a Saturday morning class, which was a big hit. By no means was it the bread and butter of our business, but I realized, that potentially, there might be a niche for kickboxing just for fitness. I realized that eight o'clock at night was actually pretty late for a workout. And people, many of them parents, still came in droves. That alone made me realize that there were "riches in niches." Many people today, especially fitness centers, try to be everything to everyone. I have found that it is better if you find one thing you are stellar at and stick with that.

During that time period when I was driving to Xavier's gym and back and thinking about what I had seen there, I noticed a women-only fitness chain called Curves had grown to ten thousand stores, the largest fitness franchise in the world. My entrepreneurial engine was revving up again. This concept really intrigued me. I loved the idea of a small space, say 1,200 square feet, and a circuit-training model, where the customer was never late to a class and could just show up and get started. That circuit-training business model that Curves used just seemed to make so much sense, given how busy people are. And the fact that the workout was only thirty minutes made the program very marketable. Once, I even went into a Curves location and pretended to be asking for information for my mother. I also had my wife call and get some information. Sometimes you just gotta do what you gotta do, right? I just *had* to learn more about how Curves ran its operations because a twist on that concept had started to form in my mind. I thought, *I could use the same circuit format that Curves uses, seeing as that isn't proprietary in and of itself, but spice it up by making it a thirty-minute* kickboxing *workout.* The potential seemed unlimited, and I soon became determined to make it work.

Our kickboxing fitness classes at the karate school had always been forty-five minutes long, but following the lead set by Curves, I knew I could find a way to pare it down to thirty minutes. That's how we got the name 9Round. It's a nine-round (station) workout with three minutes each round—altogether twenty-seven minutes. Factor in the thirty-second active breaks between rounds, and you have a thirty-minute workout. (Don't tell anyone, but it's actually thirty-one minutes!) Heather and I actually thought of several other names for the business. Golden Glove was one we sat on for a while, but it just didn't stick. 9Round felt like the right name, and I felt like a workout packaged the way I was envisioning was sure to be groundbreaking.

Kevin was not so keen on the idea. He did not want to rent another space and go into debt. We'd had financial trouble already and remember—one karate school that wasn't doing so hot. Not surprisingly, he declined to get involved. Honestly, I can't say that I blame him. It was early 2008, the economy was starting to falter, and we weren't exactly booming at the time. In fact, at this point, we were beginning to separate our three karate schools altogether, and I was buying out the third school that I'd been managing. My brother and I were severing all business ties for the first time in our lives. The way my paychecks for the first two locations were being taken away gave me and my wife only a few months until money was going to be tighter than ever. She was considering going back to work but not sure where. What kind of time was this for me to invent a new business?!

However, I had my wife's full support. I joke that it was because she didn't know how much work it was going to be. But, really, neither one of us did!

I was convinced that franchising was the right vehicle of growth for me as an entrepreneur. After all, that's what Curves had done, right? Still, I knew I had to have one store that was not only profitable but a real standout. So I needed the flagship store to be wildly successful. I learned that this venture, like so many things in business (and in life in general), was going to be an ongoing learning experience. Almost seven years later we are still learning!

However, for the time being, I had to take the plunge, get the first 9Round open, and get all the kinks out. I had to rent the space myself, and I didn't have my brother as a banker, not to mention that 9Round was an unproven concept. Making matters even more difficult, financially I was very cash poor. I had responsibilities, a growing family, and more bills than ever. It might have seemed to be too much to handle in a bad economy, but I was determined to make it work. I knew deep in my heart that there was something very big I needed to be creating in my life. Some call it instinct, some call it intuition, but I like to call it just plain ballsy.

To get 9Round off the ground, I maxed out my *one* credit card. But that wasn't going to be enough money. Every now and then, you luck up and know someone who also believes that you're brilliant. I must have proved somehow that I had a decent head on my shoulders because, the next thing I knew, a gentleman named Billy Morrow loaned me $10,000 on a handshake, telling me simply, "Pay it back as you can." He thought my inspiration for this new business made sense too and was willing to be the bank for the venture. I'd met Billy through karate, when I'd taught classes to him and his wife. It goes to show that if you treat people well in business, you never know how it may pay off. It was a handshake deal—something you just don't see happen much these days. Let me tell you, Billy and his wife have a lifetime membership with 9Round. Even though I went into debt with Billy, I knew it was the only way I could bring my vision to reality.

THE INSPIRATION COMES TO LIFE

It was pretty easy to pick out a spot for our flagship 9Round location. There was an empty space, adjacent to our third karate school, located in Greenville, and 1,127 square feet. I thought the fact that it was right next door would make both businesses easy to manage. I actually had a door cut in between the walls so I could easily check on 9Round between karate classes. The build-out was extremely minimal. Looking back at old photos, I find that it's actually pretty funny to see how minimal that first location was. We have come a long way in the past few years.

I'm not the handiest guy in the world, but I don't mind learning, working hard, and putting in long hours. I had no idea how to go about fixing Sheetrock, painting, or working with electrical stuff. I needed a contractor to build the location, so I asked the landlord if he knew a good one.

The contractor the landlord recommended was a one-man show and not the best, but he would work long hours and do exactly what I asked. He had a heart of gold. You can't ask for much more in a builder, right? Even though the work was not perfect, he really meant well, and today when I see him, he still always asks, "How many 9Rounds you got now?" He's really a great guy. I remember staying up there until midnight, helping him paint the walls, put up the decor, and lay the floor mats. We made many trips to Lowes in his old truck that smelled like an ashtray. Unfortunately for him, he smoked like an old chimney and drank two entire two-liters of Pepsi a day! Sometimes I was worried he was going to keel over on me right in the middle of the build-out. He was not the picture of health, but he was helping me build a place where health was going to be the focus.

I knew the atmosphere of the gym was going to be a key part of the experience for the members who signed up. Xavier's gym is right in line with the no-nonsense, old-school persona. The inside walls are all brick (the 9Round locations use faux brick), and he has no use for amenities such as heat or air-conditioning. One of Xavier's favorite quotes is, "The tougher in the gym, the easier in the fight." You will, however, find bloodstains on the ring and, of course, the ubiquitous jazz music always thumping through the gym's speaker system. You can hear it all the way from the parking lot. It's one heck of an experience.

When I visit Xavier's gym, I don't bring my cell phone inside. I want no distractions. An atmosphere that inspired members to have that level of focus is one of the things we have tried to emulate inside of our 9Round locations. We try to get the customer to fully unplug from the work/home life and really *focus* on his or her workout for just thirty minutes. In fact, these elements of real, hard-core training are exactly what I kept in my mind when I was creating this business model. I found the whole idea of the bricks and the place being kind of raw very appealing. I wanted to bring as much authenticity to the gym's appearance as I possibly could.

As I got inspired for the look and feel for 9Round, I was a careful to dance the line between re-creating Xavier's old-school look and feel without going so far that it was intimidating, and on the other hand, not going so modern that 9Rounds felt like any other shiny big-box gym. I wanted a more down-to-earth feel. I wanted people to have an experience when they walked in, just like I always did at Biggs's boxing gym. So posters of the greats, like Ali, Bruce Lee, and Sugar Ray Robinson adorn the walls, but we have them in uniform frames and hung exactly six bricks from the top of each panel, rather than duct-taped to the walls and peeling at the corners. Like at Xavier's gym, we have two mirrors up front. Unlike the trendy franchised gyms, at 9Round, the mirrors are not intended for you to spend time flexing and looking at your muscles, but rather to watch your form during the varying exercises performed in the club. Our club design and setup is very unique. While it is not the dirty, bloody kind of place you might see in the movies, in many ways, it does have the same energy and feel as the old-school boxing gym. I chose low lighting as well, just like you would have at an old-school gym instead of at a shiny techy facility where you go to look at others and be seen instead of to sweat. Thankfully, just about everyone else seems to like that choice too, and the women in particular (the majority of our members) really like the low lighting.

As I watch the 9Round clients work out, I can see the sweat flying, and I can hear the dancing rhythm of the speed bag and the grunts as people are taking shots to the heavy bag. Where the old-school boxing gyms were filled with amateur and professional fighters, a 9Round club is filled with moms, executives, and everyday people.

Music, something catchy and upbeat, is always playing. Our place really rocks. It is pounding, pumping, and energizing. Though I'm a huge fan of jazz and funk, we noticed this music didn't work inside a 9Round. When we opened the doors, it was my vision to play just jazz, James Brown, and old-school funk. My wife wasn't sure if that would translate well, but we tried it for several months. After enough clients said, "What's up with the music?" I finally gave in and realized that unless you've been trained by Biggs himself and experienced the fun he can create with a pumping jazz song, it probably doesn't make sense. Now we play a mix of upbeat music such as rock, R&B, dance music, and stuff like that. The music has become one of the most important elements in our 9Round atmosphere. It keeps the energy up.

OPENING DAY

This was such an exciting time for Heather and me. I called her on the way home on the night before we opened, and she asked excitedly, "How does it look?"

I said, "Honey, it looks exactly like what I had pictured in my mind. I can't believe it." It was one of the most satisfying moments of my life to that point.

While I had scraped enough money up to open, I was operating on such a shoestring budget I still could not afford essential things like a sign or marketing materials. All I could afford was a hundred-dollar banner. After our first thirty days in business, we had signed up almost one hundred members. That's when I knew we had a tiger by the tail. I said to myself, *We are going to make millions.*

KNOCKOUT NUGGETS

1. *Riches are in niches.* One of the things that will help you start your own business is finding a niche in the marketplace. I found a niche in kickboxing fitness and focused solely on that. The more moving parts a business has, the easier it is to not do *anything* well. I read that it took Tom Monaghan, the founder of Domino's, forever to add Diet Coke to the Domino's Pizza menu. He said, "It's just one more thing that could get screwed up." You can't be everything to everybody. Starbucks does one thing better than anybody—coffee. You can crush the competition by doing one thing better than anyone in your field.

2. *The borrower is slave to the lender.* One of the very first goals Heather and I had was to pay back Billy Morrow as fast as we could. Remember—he was the guy I made the handshake deal with, who helped make 9Round happen. I followed a principle that I learned from *The Richest Man in Babylon* by George Samuel Clason: every single month, I guaranteed Billy that I would pay him something. Some months it would be only $100, and some months it would be $800, but I was determined to pay him something every month. At the beginning of the year, as we do each year, Heather and I sat down and wrote out our annual goals. One of our written goals was to pay Billy Morrow off. I would physically drive to the bank and deposit money into

his account. It took us about eighteen months, but we got it done.

Here's the secret: the amount doesn't matter; it's the plan that really matters. Most people don't have a plan at all. If you have debts today, I recommend you contact the debtor and set up a payment plan and get aggressive in paying them off. Paying off a debt is a mental relief. It will free up mental space so you can focus on wealth.

3. *There is no plan B.* When my wife and I opened the doors to our first 9Round in 2008, we never thought, *What if this doesn't work?* It absolutely had to work. If you start a business, make it work. You have to dive in 100 percent. Today, when franchise candidates come to visit us, I sit them down and ask them, "Are you ready for sixty-hour workweeks? Are you ready to come home at around 9:00 p.m. and miss the kids' bedtime for a while?" If they are ready for this type of commitment, then I know they have a chance. Semi-absentee ownership just doesn't work. The franchise broker industry seems to lean toward pushing semi-absentee businesses, and 9Round is not that type of a business. We are an owner-operator model. A 9Round franchise is not an investment; it's a way of life.

4. *Knocked down seven times? Get up eight!* Putting the memories of my early business ventures down on paper made me realize that I'd never really noticed the list of failed businesses that I tried. If I were to have dwelled on those failed attempts, I could have gotten down pretty quickly. But during the times those setbacks were actually happening to me, I had an inner drive

that always stayed clear. There was just no way I was giving up on my dream of being a multimillionaire and a well-respected entrepreneur. The safe route would have been to just keep working with my brother and continue with the karate business, but I felt constrained, and I just knew in my gut there had to be more. Just because one idea doesn't work doesn't mean you shouldn't have any more ideas.

No matter what life throws at you, you must keep fighting. I say all the time that I don't need fighters or kickboxers to operate a 9Round franchise, but I do need fighters in life and in business. Part of life is understanding how to handle the bad times. Because they will always come. A good analogy is the seasons. Winter always comes after fall, and this has been the pattern since the beginning of time. As you are on your way to creating your business, don't let the winters stop you completely. If you get knocked down, get right back up.

Here I am at eight years old showing off my side kick.

Here I am again at eight years old. I had just
earned my blue belt in karate.

My brother (kneeling) and me the night I got my black belt.
I was ten years old, and this is a day I will never forget.

This is a wedding photo the day Heather and I got married at the
local courthouse. Dad is in the middle with me on the left, and my
big brother is on the right. This was May 29, 2007, and Heather and I
chose to spend what little savings we had on a honeymoon rather than
on a fancy wedding. To this day, I think it was money well spent.

Master Wei (center) was one of my many instructors throughout the years in martial arts. Master Wei was a Tai Chi master, and I was lucky to train with him for almost five years. My wife got to train with him also. He was eighty-six years old in this photograph, and he, unfortunately, passed away a few years after this photo was taken.

Amateur kickboxing was such an exhilarating experience. Competition reveals true character. In this photo, I am on the prowl with intense focus.

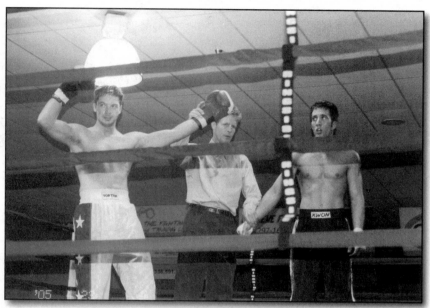

Ahhhh! The thrill of victory! In the fight world, there's only first and second place. You never want to be second place.

The Champ! Shannon "The Cannon" Hudson

Heather was eight months pregnant with Jackson in this photo.
Even though we didn't have a lot of money, we had big dreams.

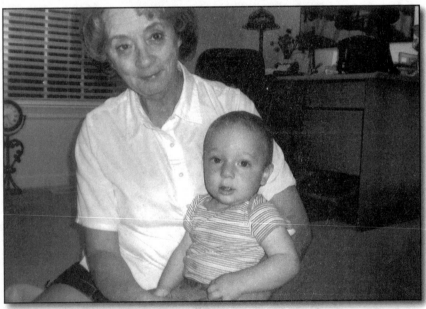

In this photo, my mom, June, was spending some precious time with
Jackson. She's an amazing woman who still practices karate each week.

Here is Jackson at Christmas in 2008.

My supersmart stepdaughter, Elana

The Hudson Family

Heather and myself at a photo shoot in 2015. We *are* a power couple.

Here is what a busy 9Round looks like. It's high energy, fun, and exciting. It's like a party—a 9Round party.

CHAPTER SEVEN

READY, FIRE ... AIM?

Can you believe it? Not even after one year of official 9Round business, I sold my first franchise. What an exciting time! There I was again, in over my head.

As I've mentioned, one of my shortcomings is my instinct for readying, firing, and then realizing I forgot to aim rather than first taking aim. I do things extremely quickly—sometimes without doing all my homework first. Heather can, at times, be somewhat the same way, yet she is more deliberate, more precise. I can pull the trigger fast, and she can too. But she goes about it in a more intelligent manner. I learn from her too.

FRANCHISING

Before I opened the first physical location of 9Round, my strategy was to license the concept inside the big-box gyms. So luckily, I landed an interview to unveil the concept at a local big box in my town. I was really prepared. I had a quick DVD made featuring how awesome kickboxing was for health and fitness. I even had an attorney friend who agreed to come along with me. This gave me some much-needed confidence. I needed all the confidence I could get because I was going to present in front of the CEO and his team.

Immediately when the meeting started, things went wrong. The guy hadn't signed a confidentiality agreement to keep my idea secret, which he was supposed to have signed before the meeting. I had sent it to him about a week in advance. He refused to sign it. What a prick! Then he basically laughed at my decor. He said, "We have fifty-dollar light bulbs from Italy. I'm not putting up cheap brick paneling in my clubs." I was discouraged, but I did not give up because I knew I had the experience and that I knew how to make this concept work. So that meeting concluded, and I was flat out rejected. That's when I shifted strategies and decided to make a stand-alone brick-and-mortar 9Round location. Massive success is the best revenge. I was determined to make 9Round work!

I was always thinking: Is this scalable—meaning, can this work throughout one hundred–plus locations? When you are building your first location (assuming you want to start your own business or already have) here are some good questions to ask yourself.

1. Can I duplicate this concept?
2. Will it appeal to the masses?
3. Can I train the staff quickly and efficiently?
4. Will it eventually run without my physical presence?
5. Is my logo and name sign friendly and catchy?
6. Can I tell someone in twenty seconds or less what the business is?

If you answered yes to these questions, then you have a business that can be franchised or licensed. In the next chapter, I am going to tell you exactly how I franchised 9Round. After all, that was the goal from the beginning. Let me first tell you about my first franchisee.

THE FIRST FRANCHISEE

My first franchisee was a man named Iain Robson, a really nice guy in his late forties and also one of our members. A retired CPO who'd served for twenty years in the US Navy, Iain fell in love with the concept of 9Round and would often tell me how terrific he thought it was. He took his training seriously and would come in three or four times a week and work out very hard. You can tell a lot about a person when you watch him or her train. Iain was an intense, no-nonsense guy, and knew how to execute a plan, probably thanks to his military background. He had no kids still living at home with him, and when he decided that he wanted to open up his own franchise, he knew that he would be able to devote himself full-time to the business.

And here it is again—ready, fire, oops. Iain kept urging me to sign him up as my first franchisee. He and I met several times and got to know, like, and trust each other. In fact, he worked part-time on Saturdays for me too. He was ready to be the first franchisee immediately. It was just that, on my end, I wasn't. I didn't yet have the legal documents prepared to set up a franchisee, but he was eager to come on board, and I was equally eager to have him and begin proving the concept could easily be duplicated.

One of the reasons for his urgency was his job. It was repairing pay phones and also emptying quarters from the phones. With the ubiquity of cell phones, that job was, of course, becoming obsolete very fast. He didn't really like the work anyway, and more important, he was sick of it and was ready for something more challenging. He was ready for an exciting new business venture and to become his own boss. This was a great opportunity for him; he would be the first franchisee in the infancy stages of the 9Round system.

We met at a coffee shop called Java Jolt in our retail strip. We talked about getting started, but I told him I didn't have the money to complete the legal process that would enable me to take on franchisees. But I had an idea. I said, "If you pay just ten thousand dollars for the franchise, you will be the first franchisee."

Paying the ten grand up front would not only give Iain a discount start-up price; he would get in on the ground floor, lock in a royalty of only $300 a month (today the fee is more), and pay no national marketing/branding fee. What a steal, right? So he agreed and wrote a check. I then went to Dave Waldman, of a company called The Franchise Maker, and got all the legal stuff finished up. In fact, I needed that $10,000 from Iain to pay Dave so he could finish up the franchise agreement. I had researched three or four companies to help me get all the legal documents ready to franchise, and Dave seemed to be a very understanding, likeable guy, who could relate to where I was in the launch of the 9Round brand. So of course, I quickly jumped on board and secured his consulting services. It helped that he had a pay-as-you-go program because cash was tight for me and Heather at the time. In fact, if he hadn't had that program, I'm not sure how I would have gotten the money together.

When Iain opened his doors in a store about ten miles away from me, he got off to a good start and was signing up thirty to forty members a month. In the meantime, the documents were done. But I neglected to ever have him sign a franchise agreement. That was a bad decision. In retrospect, it really wasn't a decision, but rather an inability to make a decision, and that inability would rock the boat. Remember Iain was my first "franchisee," so to speak, and I wanted him to have a smooth rollout. However, mostly because of my reluctance to upset things, I now had my very first franchisee running a franchise with no legal agreement! All we had between us was a handshake agreement. I didn't want to force the issue, but eventually things got dicey between Iain and me.

Today, 9Round is nothing like it was in 2008 or 2009. Everything is so much more robust and organized now. And that's exactly the way it should be; in business you either evolve or die. I take pride on being a company that is always evolving and looking three to five years into the future. The problem with Iain was that he would not change or evolve. For example, we implemented changes to the software, but he didn't want to go along with the changes. He didn't appreciate change, but rather was very stuck in his ways. Since I had no franchise agreement to enforce, I couldn't require him to conform. I tried to convince and reason with him about the needed changes, but he was stubborn, and he didn't like the speed of change.

In the franchise industry, it is said that being the first franchisee is a blessing and a curse. You get in early, but on the other hand, you see a lot of change. Iain and I got into arguments, and there were other problems too. I think ego had a lot to do with it. I was a young entrepreneur and the CEO, but that didn't seem to matter to him. He wasn't about to take orders or suggestions from me without a signed franchise agreement.

When his shop started to decline and sales began to fall, he went dark on me and wouldn't communicate. However, rather than take the bull by the horns and solve the problem decisively, once and for all, I instead took the path of least resistance. That went on until 2012 when Iain decided that he wanted out. He lawyered up, and that, of course, forced me to do the same. I was thinking, *Oh great, lawyers. Here we go!*

Iain and his lawyer's claim was that I hadn't followed the Federal Trade Commission guidelines. And they were right. He never had been fully disclosed of the opportunity with what is known as an FDD (Franchise Disclosure Document), and he never signed a franchise agreement.

Consequently, he wanted me to refund the entire $40,000 that he'd invested into his store, along with lawyer fees. When it was all over in an out of court settlement, it cost me a total of $80,000, including all lawyer fees. Talk about an expensive lesson! I took the store over in 2013 and chalked it up to my early lack of experience.

Thankfully, we have a much better and more sophisticated system in place today. I would now never let a new franchise open up without a solid and standardized agreement firmly in place. You readers out there, if you don't get anything from this book, at least get this. If you are in any kind of business, put everything, and I mean everything, in writing. Listen, my word is my wand, and it's as pure as gold. If I say it, then that's what I do. However, the other party doesn't always believe in that philosophy. People with the best intentions might remember things differently or not be quite sure what they agreed to. So it's safer for everyone involved if it's written down, "codified," and signed off on. Do I like it? No. But that's the way it has to be these days.

As far as Iain and me, the way we parted ways was unfortunate. My first franchise experience was a lesson in dotting the i's and crossing the t's. And it was a lesson about having the confidence to enforce the standards. Heather and

I didn't have the guts to say, "It needs to be done like this." We learned quickly that you have to be very strict on franchisees, or they will go off on tangents of who knows what. Again, I think I can trace the whole fiasco back to my impulse to shoot first and then take aim. It's one thing to move quickly, but it is another to act hastily or sloppily. You can't be careless, especially when you consider that, in business, things get more complicated the bigger you get.

FRANCHISING TODAY

Because 9Round is so much bigger now, I can't get involved on a personal level with every franchisee. That's a double-edged sword. All my friends are franchisees, and I can, therefore, no longer deal with them solely as friends. This is both good and bad. If they are doing things wrong, I have to get on them and act like a parent. Two good friends who are both now franchisees come to mind. One is one of my best buddies, Brian. Brian and I trained together, kickboxed competitively together, and went to school together. And another is my longtime karate buddy Jerry. Brian and I first met when we were both in sixth grade. We grew up together. Shortly after 9Round started growing quickly, Brian and his family bought in. Now they have three locations. Jerry owns a 9Round in Knoxville, Tennessee. When I went out to dinner with Brian recently, he didn't want to talk business … at least not initially. But you guessed it; before the evening was over, we were talking about business!

Of course, I don't know the out-of-state franchisees as well. It's not that I don't want to get to know people; I do. But there is a delicate balance between being a likable friend and still being respected when you have to put your foot down. At the 2014 9Round Annual Convention, I was giving my presentation about the future of the company. At the end, because I am sincere about being available to everybody, I put my personal cell phone number up on the big screen. I told them, "If you have a problem and you're not getting the attention or an answer you need, call me." I know that lots of CEOs say things like that but don't mean it and don't practice the promise either. But I wanted to show the franchise owners that I genuinely do care and that I'm there to help them.

The bottom line is—and I don't care how corny this may sound—I want to be known as a businessman who really cares, because I do. That's not only a reflection of who I am and how my mind works. It's also smart business.

In the next chapter, you will see how we really started getting some traction in the franchise industry. Hold on to your seats for this roller-coaster ride!

KNOCKOUT NUGGETS

1. *Know, like, and trust.* As the old saying goes, "People don't care how much you know. They only want to know how much you care." Even though I have won a world title kickboxing professionally, I am a fifth-degree black belt, I have a college degree, and I've been a personal trainer, people never just hand over $18,000 and say, "Here's my money. Give me a 9Round franchise." It never works like that. People want to know how solid the company is and, more importantly, how solid the leadership is. They want to know if I am going to help them be a success and whether I really give a rip. They are also wondering if I have the tools to help them. One of the lessons I learned a good while back is that people will not buy from you until they get to *know, like,* and *trust* you. When you start your own business, remember that lesson.

- *Know* – Potential customers have to get to know you as a person and what you stand for. Let customers know your background and why you are in the business you are in. Everyone has a story, and the more a customer can relate to you and yours, the better the business relationship will be. You can easily tell your story and share who you are as a person via a website or brochure that any potential business associates or customers can easily access.

- *Like* – Potential business associates will buy from you more easily if you are likable. So work on your personality, your smile, your handshake, your communication, your writing, and your speech. Work hard on yourself. *You* are *it!* You might want to circle that short sentence or put a star beside it.

- *Trust* – Trust will be easily gained if you have the knowledge/education and skills about your product or service and can demonstrate and communicate them. Always read and learn. How do you reach the good stuff on the higher shelves in life? You have to stand on the books you have read, right?

2. *Write everything down.* Getting things in writing is crucial when you're in business with someone because it's the only way to know what people are responsible for. This principle is also useful in your personal life. Writing stuff down has really helped me in the last few

years. It's so easy to forget even the simplest things. I'm a pen and paper kind of guy. To-do lists and having a calendar have saved my butt many times. As your business and life get more and more complex, the best way to keep track and stay on top of it all is to write down the things you want and need to do, so the list can serve as a reminder to do those things. The simple act of checking things off makes you feel productive. I absolutely love checking off the list as I go through the day. Also, writing down creative ideas has helped me. So I write more than just a to-do list. I write ideas for big projects that I might want to do later. I still have my notes on the company I run today, and it's fun to see the skeleton of ideas jotted down way before they were actually anything tangible. Scientists say that the average person has sixty thousand thoughts go through his or her mind every day. There is no way to remember all of them. So if an idea excites you, write it down.

3. *Mistakes, mistakes, mistakes.* One of the things you have to get your head around if you are going to be a business leader is that you will make mistakes. In fact, you will make a lot of them, especially in the beginning. I made a few mistakes early because of my ready, fire, aim approach. A great analogy for this lesson is baseball. You have to cover all the bases but with speed. The mistake I made was selling the franchise to Iain without having a franchise agreement in place. In other words, I didn't cover all the bases first. You can't make a home run without touching first, second, and third base.

   The mistakes I made with my first franchisee were pretty bad, and luckily we had the money to pay it off and get out of the jam. If the company had not been financially strong enough, that one mistake could have sunk us. But Heather and I have always been very smart with our finances. Don't beat yourself up too badly when you make a mistake. Just learn from it and keep moving forward. Treat it like a speed bump in the road. You don't come to a complete stop. You just slow down a bit. And once you are over it, you speed up and you're on your way. Be ready for the speed bumps and don't ever stop! Learn from them and continue on toward your goal.

CHAPTER EIGHT

THE SAGE

I knew that I wanted to grow my business by adding on new franchisees, but I also realized that, realistically, there was only so much that I could do on my own. It was 2010, a couple of years had gone by since we opened our first 9Round location, and we were plucking along pretty well at that time. We had about ten locations open, all which were sold organically. What I mean by that is the owners were members first, fell in love with the concept, and purchased the franchise. I figured that another way to reach out to a wider field of candidates would be to engage a broker to make the pitch for me.

Like real estate brokers, franchise business brokers don't earn their money unless they are successful in actually selling a new franchise for you. The broker groups like to joke that they eat what they kill. The commission is usually a portion of the initial franchise fee that ranges anywhere from 33 percent to 100 percent. It really surprised me when I found out what these brokers made. I thought for a minute, *Maybe I'm in the wrong business!* Why would I give up such a large percentage of the initial franchise fee, which at that time, we so desperately needed? What I know now is how important it is to bring the *right* owner into the organization. This is crucial to an organization's longevity. We can't just sell to anyone who has the money and can fog a mirror. If a broker group is what I need to bring in the right operator, and they get a hefty fee, then so what? It's a win-win for everyone. The broker makes money. I have a great operator. And even though we don't make much on the initial franchise fee, we make the real money on the back end with royalties and equipment sales. And because we are choosy about our operators, we get good ones, many of whom soon open more locations. I want to build a brand that will be around long after I am gone, so we have got to have strong, brand-loyal operators.

Not sure exactly where to look for a broker, I took the route of all modern day entrepreneurs and scoured the Internet. Before long, my search paid off, and I found an organization called the Franchise Broker Association. I reached out to the organization and arranged for a conference call that would allow me to pitch the concept to the group. This was my big chance to *wow* them and get them excited about 9Round. I had no clue how to structure a call like this, so I just dove in and spoke from the heart. It was a thirty-minute conference call, and keenly aware of the somewhere between twenty and thirty people who were listening, I was rather nervous and probably talking a bit too rapidly during my presentation. For me, that call was more nerve-racking than stepping into the ring to fight had ever been. I was afraid of having any dead air, so I just kept enthusiastically talking! When I hung up, I really had no clue what I had just said or whether any of it made any sense.

But it only takes one person to transform an enterprise. If I could inspire one broker with franchise experience, wisdom, and the ambition to be a success, then 9Round could grow even faster. As things turned out, a man (we will call him Mr. Broker) called and pitched his services to me. He explained that he had been in the franchise industry for thirty years and had a law degree from Stanford. Overall, he sounded very impressive. He even volunteered to come visit me from his home base up north on his own dime. Eager to find out more about how Mr. Broker could help me, I agreed.

Mr. Broker visited me in South Carolina, and we got along well. My initial impression was that he was a "fuddy-duddy" in his late fifties. He always wore khakis and a sweater tied over his shoulders and had glasses and white fluffy hair. However, it was obvious that he definitely knew his stuff. And when it came to all the intricacies and finer points of franchising, I really needed some solid guidance. For me and Heather, these were completely uncharted waters. I didn't know anything about law, but I knew that Stanford was a great school. I figured that this was just what the doctor ordered—a tried and true professional who could move my company to the next level. I agreed to have him work as a broker for 9Round to help expand our franchising on a commission only basis.

Mr. Broker offered to review the franchise agreement that I was using, and long story short, he basically talked us into doing a lot of deal making—something we had not done initially. For example, a prospective franchisee might need more time to open the store, perhaps six additional months. So Mr. Broker would create an addendum to the agreement. Or it could be that the franchisee-to-be wanted a larger territory for the store or a first right of refusal. A first right of refusal simply means that if someone wanted to put a 9Round location in a particular area, we had to first approach the current nearby owner and see if he or she wanted it. If he or she declined it, then it was fair game for a new buyer. The bottom line was, we came to the point where virtually every agreement had an addendum. Heather and I wondered if this was normal. Mr. Broker convinced us that it was indeed normal and that since we were a new company, we had to wheel and deal to get on the map. Heather was the first one who spoke up. I remember her saying, "We aren't a flea market where you haggle deals!" Boy, what great intuition she has. She has the uncanny ability to sniff out bad character.

Another element Mr. Broker introduced into our business (and another example of how, I believe, he led us astray) was selling area rights. What that means is someone could purchase the right to develop an entire area—the area rights—and in turn, he or she would get a split of the up-front franchise fees and royalties throughout that area. One of our craziest deals ever was selling the rights to an entire state. That's right. One owner has an entire state! Although he is required to open a store every six months for the next ten years, the advantage is still his. He either has to sell a franchise or open a new store himself. Now I realize I don't need an area developer. Each month when I stroke the check to the area developer it gives me heartburn because I can't unwind the deal. That's what the agreement says, and that's what I agreed to. I'm stuck with it. We have ten units in the state, with another three or four sold and in the works. I still have the same arrangement today. He's doing what he's supposed to, so I can't get out of it, and it's frustrating. Don't get me wrong, the area developer is a great guy and did nothing wrong. Hindsight is always twenty-twenty, right? He got a hell of a deal.

Because of Mr. Broker's strategies, Heather and I are now saddled with a number of (what should have been) avoidable commitments that we have to stick to even though they are not favorable to us. Yes, to some extent I will concede Mr. Broker's point—we were new and, to a point, remaining flexible was a necessity. But by the same token, I am convinced that we were far too generous with some of the addendums that we granted. Moreover, Mr. Broker's commission was very gracious. He would get all the leads and half of each eighteen thousand-dollar franchise fee. It was one heck of a good run for him. He got all the leads, which we paid for and provided, and in one year, he banked commissions that totaled a whopping $300,000—at a time when Heather and I were struggling to make the house payment. Actually, we didn't take our first salary from the business until May 2013, a full four years after we started franchising. Prior to that, we always put everything back into the company for growth and infrastructure.

Was it that Mr. Broker himself really didn't know how things worked? I still wonder about that today. This book, of course, is in large part based on giving advice through hindsight. My advice is don't be ignorant about the process. I didn't know how much brokers normally get paid or how a true sales process should work in a franchised business. Because of my propensity for "ready, fire, aim," I jumped right into the arrangement with Mr. Broker too quickly. Maybe I move too quickly, but I have a great business intuition. Don't be ignorant about the processes that are pertinent to your craft. I was ignorant about creating amendments, addendums, what's fair, and what's normal in the franchise industry. Today, I know a lot more about what's on the up-and-up in the franchise broker world. So learn your stuff first, and ask a ton of questions. Don't just assume that because someone claims to be an expert in a particular field he or she actually is an expert. Few decisions are clear when you are in charge of a business. Sometimes a decision has positives and negatives, but the decisions you make should make sense, even if they don't always make you comfortable. There's a time for gathering information and a time for action, and mistakes are part of the process. Even though making decisions is tough, that's what keeps things exciting and adventurous. I love the thrill of having to make big decisions. That's what being an entrepreneur is all about. When you don't have tough decisions to make, you're not making much progress.

That time period of about a year and a half when we were following Mr. Broker's advice was a great year of growth and learning for us. It is said that you are going to feel uncomfortable when you are growing. That's exactly how Heather and I feel almost every day. But it's a story that is as old as business itself. We were rookies, and Mr. Broker was a highly experienced veteran. He had been in the business for thirty years and had worked for some famous brands, including a big hotel chain, among many others. I had no reason to doubt any of what he was telling me. But we were so green that we just didn't know what we didn't know. Don't get me wrong. We resisted a lot of the addendums. I'd say, "This is crazy." But then Mr. Broker would go to work and persuade us to go along with what he was asking. I'm sure that, in almost every instance, his guiding principle was simple: Let's get the sale no matter what it takes.

I guess in some sense, Mr. Broker's actions demonstrate what's at the heart of any business relationship. He was acting, within the parameters we had established, on his own behalf.

As far as he was concerned, whether or not those parameters were in our best interest was our business. It wasn't affecting *his* bottom line to slip in an addendum that didn't necessarily benefit us, because, after the sale, he wasn't the one who would have to live with the deal. The situation is summed up well by one of my favorite jokes: the brokers get to have the sex, but we have to raise the kids!

Having said all that, entrepreneurs often have no choice other than to work with brokers or a sales group, no matter how reluctantly. You need them to get some traction, but never forget that, for the most part, any sales personnel you hire are looking out for themselves and not for the brand that you as the founder are trying so hard to establish and promote. You can't expect them to always be on the exact same page as you. Of course, there are good brokers and bad ones, and the good ones clearly understand that bringing in the right person to a franchised organization is key. The bad ones don't vet the candidate out and make sure the fit is correct, not just for the candidate but also for the franchise chain. Unfortunately, there are many who just want to make a quick buck and will sell to anyone who will fog a mirror. The good ones who are honest and understand this philosophy can help an organization grow very quickly.

I discuss staffing more in chapter ten, but the takeaway point is that even when you hire someone to help you, you can't lose sight of what will ultimately lead to success—the right people. Heather and I had to continue to figure out how to do that ourselves as we moved forward.

KNOCKOUT NUGGET

1. *Take heavy action.* The ready, fire, aim strategy can be a great quality for entrepreneurs. In fact, I think all the greats have that trait in them. I see so many people who want to own their own business and live the American dream but are just unable to pull the trigger. They have what I like to call, "paralysis by analysis." They will

analyze pro forma data and spreadsheets until they are blue in the face. When Heather and I started 9Round, we didn't have a formal business plan and never even heard of the word *pro forma*. Balance sheet? Profit and loss sheet? What were those things? All I knew was that we needed more money coming in than going out. Sometimes keeping things simple is the key in business.

2. *Things don't just happen; they happen just.* Sometimes you have to go through tough learning experiences to get to the next level. In fact, I don't think Heather and I could have avoided the entanglement we got into with Mr. Broker. After all, we were the owners, and we did agree to let Mr. Broker have all the leads and make a nine thousand-dollar commission on each sale. We became pretty close in the year and a half Mr. Broker worked with us. He was like family, and Heather nicknamed him Papa 9Round at one time. He even drove to Canada and watched me win my world title. Today we don't speak, and I hate that. The way the situation ended was tough, and you will read exactly how it ended in the next chapter, but again, it was one of those lessons that we needed to learn. I learned that things happen for a reason.

3. *Ignorance is not bliss.* When you want to move quickly in business, you had better know what you are doing. Think about it this way: if you had to have a surgical procedure done, you would hope the surgeon operating on you knew every piece of knowledge available about the operation. When you decide to jump into your business, study, read books, take courses, ask questions,

and seek out a mentor. It doesn't matter how you learn every detail about your business; you just need to learn it. As Jim Rohn, who is one of my favorite speakers, said, "In five years, you will surely arrive. The question is, where?"

CHAPTER NINE

THE 24-7 GYM MAFIA

Despite our mistakes, our momentum was building. I just knew we would get noticed in the franchise world for what we were doing. We had thirty-six locations open and *Entrepreneur* magazine picked us to be listed in its prestigious Franchise 500 list. We were ranked number 443 in the January 2013 issue. I know people don't chant, "We are number 2!" But Heather and I were chanting "443!" all day when we got the news.

One day in January 2013, I got a call from a man named Gary Findley, who explained that he was the COO of a major franchise in the fitness industry. This franchise operated 24-7 facilities that were around three thousand square feet and offered key card access, cardio equipment, free weights, an aerobics room, and numerous other amenities. Its business model was totally different from that of 9Round, but it was still in the fitness space. At the time, the franchise had 1,400 stores in seven countries. Clearly, this was a major player in the fitness and franchise industry, and I was of course quite flattered to hear from the franchise.

I wasn't personally familiar with the chain because none of its locations were in my area. But the bigwigs at the 24-7 chain evidently were very familiar with 9Round and liked our business model and what we were doing. They had obviously done extensive research on us, or else they wouldn't have been calling me.

After the initial introductions, what I heard next was jaw-dropping for me. Gary told me that he had formerly been with Curves. In fact, he was with the company from its second unit all the way until it had eight thousand units—an unimaginable number to me. Wow! Frankly, I was in awe. The phenomenal success of Curves had always been one the primary inspirations for my own franchise, and now the man who was in large part responsible for that success was interested in *doing business with me.* In many ways, his call literally felt like a dream come true.

Gary was a Texas native with a southern drawl, though he now lived up north near the headquarters of the 24-7 chain, and I picked up on his accent right away. My first impulse was to think that some sort of collaboration with these guys was exactly what I needed. At the time, 9Round had only thirty-six stores. Moreover, Heather and I were growing increasingly unhappy with Mr. Broker, and I was stressed out to the max and needing a change. Not only was Mr. Broker encouraging us to include addendum after addendum, but he was forgetting to follow up with prospects, and he couldn't keep up with the volume. I remembered that he had once said to me, "I learned a long time ago, you have to follow the money." The statement was a huge red flag. When it came down to it, Heather and I just needed some guidance and direction from someone who had already done what we were doing. So this was an exciting and potentially very promising phone call.

Then Gary said, "Well, Shannon, we think you've done a great job considering your experience and time in the franchise industry, so we would like to offer you a partnership." It was one of those times that I knew a quick response would be amateurish on my part. So I asked him what he had in mind, and he said that a good first step would be for the CEO and founder of the 24-7 gym to come and visit. I readily accepted.

When we finally met, I discovered that Mr. CEO was very savvy, an excellent communicator, and an overall sharp guy. He flew down to South Carolina on a Monday night. I picked him up at his hotel, and we went to dinner, where we had an hour-long conversation. He asked me how I'd started the concept, and I enjoyed the chance to brag a little. On the other hand, it was also nice to vent to him about certain frustrations of the business, first and foremost my concerns with Mr. Broker and the addendum issue. Mr. CEO was a very personable guy with a quick mind and an approach that involved rapid talking.

The next morning I picked him up again, and this time we went to meet with Heather and toured 9Round. We discussed a multitude of topics regarding our business and franchising.

After a thorough inspection, he said, "Shannon, I like your operation, and I'd like to make you an offer."

I waited, almost holding my breath.

"First of all, we need operational control of the business," he said. "That's a must, meaning we will need at least 51 percent."

Heather and I both knew that was a deal breaker. Regardless of what or how much they offered, there was absolutely no way we were going to give up control of 9Round. This was a business that we had founded, and we had invested countless amounts of blood, sweat, and tears into it. This was, and still is, our baby. We did not come to a deal that day, and after we wrapped up, I drove Mr. CEO to the airport. I told him we would think about his offer, but I reassured him we were not going to give up operational control. For both of us, gut instinct told Heather and I this was not going to be their final offer. We knew the 24-7 chain wanted to be a part of 9Round.

Gary, the former Curves guy, seemed to understand our doubts, and as a resolution said, "I want you to come see the 24-7 corporate office."

I had a strong feeling that I would be impressed and that one visit was worth a thousand words. As it turned out, by coincidence, I had a 9Round opening near the office, so arrangements for such a visit were quickly made.

I'll never forget my shock at the weather up north. It was freezing cold the day of my visit; the high was negative nine— not what we're accustomed to down in South Carolina! I spent the day with my new 9Round club owner, and that evening, Gary picked me up and showed me around the 24-7 headquarters.

The 24-7 operation was a jaw-dropper—very impressive and cutting edge. That evening, Gary took me to dinner. When he insisted on 51 percent, I flatly turned down the offer. I stuck to my guns. I wasn't trying to be a hard-nosed negotiator; what was guiding me was simple—no way was I was going to become an employee in my own business.

So after some back and forth, we settled on 24-7 buying 40 percent. Heather and I spent many nights doing some serious pillow talk—and not the sexy kind. In fact, we spent many sleepless nights. Our minds were filled with the doubtful thoughts and questions that inevitable come with a prospect like the one we were facing. *Are we doing the right thing? Should we ask for more money? Should we even sell at all?*

How is the corporate staff going to react to this? How is the entire chain going to react?

After we signed the papers, the 24-7 chain would pay the majority of its investment up front, with the balance due when we opened our hundredth location. I'm a big fan of performance-based pay, so I said, "No problem." I knew we would get to one hundred locations pretty quickly.

You might be asking, "What happened to Mr. Broker?" Well, to put it bluntly, he was immediately axed. As Mr. CEO and Gary put it, his "gravy train" ride was over. Heather and I were relieved to find out that our gut reaction about all the crazy concessions *had been* right after all. There was no need for any changes to the franchise agreement. There was no need for silly addendums or amendments. I was silently listening in on the phone when the firing went down. Of course Mr. Broker was blindsided and mad as hell. I was ready for Mr. Broker to lawyer up. *Here we go,* I thought.

But as it turned out, he never did press or sue me. Maybe he knew he was doing something he shouldn't have and figured he had pushed the envelope far enough already. If, deep down, he thought I had wronged him, he would have lawyered up and fought. More than anything, Heather and I were disappointed, and our hearts were heavy during that time. It was like finding out your spouse was cheating on you. We had this *hurt* in our gut that felt terrible. The final straw was when Heather sent a heartfelt e-mail to Mr. Broker and asked him, "Did you really mean to hurt us?" The e-mail was really from the heart, as Heather is extremely caring about other's feelings. The e-mail also had a few other deep, burning questions, and to this day, he never answered.

Though the parting was sad and very unsettling, Heather and I now were able to buy the house of our dreams. We used a majority of the money from the partnership as a down payment on our new home. Our goal for that year was to be able to move closer to work and purchase our dream house. Using visualization, goal setting, and prayer, it happened. If your *why* is big enough the *how* will show up and get you there. We had previously been living in a 1,200-square foot house with a family of four. I still own the house today and rent it out. It's a great property, but our new house in a quiet suburb of Greenville, South Carolina, is much nicer!

TO DO AND NOT DO

With this new partnership we could network with two fantastic minds of the franchising world Mr. CEO and Gary Findley, the former Curves executive. Everyone needs a coach and a trainer or a mentor. This was my way to get mentored and learn about the franchise business. It was a super exciting time for both me and Heather. However, I did not consult an attorney or anybody else when we signed on with the 24-7 franchise, which was a big mistake. We had a purchase agreement that seemed pretty simple, and I figured that I didn't need a lawyer. It was only a few pages long and pretty easy to understand.

The operating agreement—in which you outline who does what and who is responsible for what—was a little trickier. To finalize this agreement, I pulled in my two local lawyers. Of course, we should have had them look at the purchase agreement *and* the operating agreement before we signed anything. The latter actually wasn't started until *after* we were in the partnership, and getting it hammered out took us eight months. There were disagreements about everything. The 24-7 executives even balked at the small $36,000 a year salary that Heather and I were going to take. One time, the 24-7 lawyer said, "Why do you need so much money?" I was thinking, *Are you kidding me?*

Meanwhile, we were simultaneously working and growing, using some of the 24-7 chain's vast resources.

Within the first few months of the new partnership, we found out exactly how this large company really ran behind the scenes. We were very unpleasantly surprised. For starters, Mr. CEO and his chain nickel-and-dimed me for just about everything. And as it turned out, the company's intentions for 9Round were very different from what I'd assumed them to be. The franchise intended to use 9Round as an additional profit source for their services. They wanted to sell their marketing services, legal services, and the list goes on and on, to 9Round. I understand that the name of the game is making money, but I had assumed the franchise would make most of its money from being a 40 percent equity partner, not from us purchasing their services on top of that.

On the other hand, the 24-7 mafia did bring in some very good salespeople—one of whom, in particular, is absolutely incredible. Jeff Mathews lives in Scottsdale, Arizona, and he eats, sleeps, and breathes the 9Round brand. He was and still is a franchise sales veteran and had previously been selling for the 24-7 chain. As I write this, he has sold almost two hundred locations for the 9Round brand, and today he is a very good friend. The great thing is he is now fully devoted to 9Round.

Once Jeff had started selling a lot of locations for us, we naturally started speaking on the phone quite a bit. The 24-7 office would tell him, "Don't get too close to Shannon." Heather, Jeff, and myself would wonder, *Why?* Now I see they just wanted to maintain control of everything, even who we were talking to. The smoke and mirrors just kept getting weirder and weirder.

The 24-7 staff was extremely difficult and disrespectful to me, my wife, and my team in South Carolina. Everything— from how they spoke with us on the phone to e-mails—was a constant battle. Heather and I felt a pit in our stomach, like we had been punched in the gut. This partnership wasn't what we had hoped.

We felt similarly disrespected when Mr. CEO formed his parent company and threw 9Round under it. Mr. CEO decided to start an umbrella company to house all the brands he had an interest in. That wasn't a crime, but the way he went about it was what really pissed me off. He never told us he was forming this parent company, and one day I saw the 9Round logo on his new website. To the public, it looked like Mr. CEO and the 24-7 chain owned all of 9Round, when that was not the case. When I went to the biggest franchise trade show of the year in New York City and saw the 24-7 display, I was boiling mad. The display only featured 9Round in a very small section. But right over the 9Round section, Mr. CEO was listed as the founder. I was furious. All I could think about was the story in the Bible when Jesus, angry that people were being overcharged and taken advantage of, started flipping over the tables. I wanted to flip over the tables of the whole booth in New York so badly, but I kept my cool. Yes, Mr. CEO was the founder of his parent company. But he was not the founder of 9Round.

My biggest issue was how I found out about things like this. As I said, he never mentioned anything to me about forming a parent company—and this was the problem. He should have come to me, explained what he wanted to do, and asked if he could put my trademark under his umbrella company. Of course, that never happened. If he would have respected my opinion and come to me with his plans and ideas, like a true partner should, then things would have gone a lot smoother.

Communication is the key to any partnership, and this was a prime example of an utter lack of communication.

Fast-forward to our first quarterly board meeting up north on a cold November day back in 2013. Heather and I were flying up together, and the board member we were coordinating with kept insisting that they pick us up in a warm car. Heather and I always liked to rent a car, so we could visit other 9Round locations and not have to rely on anyone else to get around. But the 24-7 chain kept pushing, saying, "You shouldn't do that. We can send a nice warm car. You won't have to deal with the traffic or the hassle of renting a car." This went on and on. And we both had a really strange feeling in our guts. We thought, *Are Mr. CEO and his crew going to drive us into a dark alley and try to kill us?* We ended up renting a car. Looking back, maybe we should have taken the offer, but that's just how much we didn't trust anyone at 24-7 at that time.

The night before the meeting, we both didn't sleep well. We really weren't sure how this meeting would go, but we were ready to fight. I felt like I was preparing for a world title fight all over again, but this time the stakes were higher—I'd be fighting for the company.

Surprisingly, the meeting went well. Mr. CEO acknowledged that when it came to 9Round, Heather and I were the leaders, and he seemed to finally give us the respect we felt we deserved. He even insisted on communicating more with us, which gave us a sense of relief. Shortly after we returned back home to South Carolina, the smoke-and-mirror show began *again*! Here are some other examples of how 24-7 would charge me extra for its services.

- If a 9Round franchise was sold, the 24-7 chain would bill me for the use of its people, even though 24-7 was a 40 percent owner of my company! For the sale of one store, the sales rep would get $5,000, and the 24-7 chain would bill be for another $2,500. Even though the sales team was good and got the job done, I resented the obvious double-dipping on the part of 24-7. I was still very involved with the sales, since I did a lot of training and preparation work with the new prospects. The 24-7 executives were operating under the mistaken belief that 9Round was like Curves and they could sell franchises to basically anyone—regardless of the potential owner's qualifications. That wasn't part of my model. My concept was unique, and it takes a special type of person to make this business model work.

- The chain would charge me $10,000 a month to use its marketing department. None of these things were in the agreement, but Mr. CEO was a good salesman and wound up convincing me to use these extra services. Mr. CEO would say, "You don't need a legal department. We have one. By the way, that will be another $10,000 per month."

So by using all 24-7's so-called *services*, we were paying anywhere between $50,000 and $100,000 a month to a company that already held a 40 percent ownership stake in my company. That really rankled me, and it just didn't sit right. On top of that, I did a little research on the 24-7 chain and Mr. CEO, and I discovered a few things that really were startling. I couldn't believe some of the things that I found. I Googled the company's name and the name of the founder (it's amazing what you can find with a simple Google search) and found lawsuit after lawsuit and complaint after complaint.

There were and still are tons of dissatisfied franchisees who vent on forums on the Internet. Trust me—they are easy to find.

Once I'd made these discoveries, Heather and I had many sleepless nights. I just kept thinking, *What have I gotten myself into?*

So my recommendation is that you have to do your research. And don't just do it on your own. Speak with others in the industry about the person you are thinking of getting in bed with, and get a lawyer to do some homework on your new potential business associate and his or her past. This is invaluable.

After about a year of that battle, I stopped paying 24-7's fees and started to pull everything back to South Carolina. We stopped using any of the 24-7 services. Heather and I want to keep all aspects of the business close to our chests so we can keep an eye on everything. Since we'd kept 60 percent ownership, we could easily pull those services and resources back down to South Carolina without 24-7's permission. Not surprisingly, the 24-7 executives were none too happy about that.

To be fair, I will acknowledge that there were ways in which I did need 24-7 to make more money. For example, the chain did source equipment, such as boxing gloves and originally did the pick, pack, and shipping from the 24-7 headquarters. The company agreed to outsource the gloves overseas, warehouse them, ship them, handle the inventory controls, and so on. I wasn't able to fund $100,000 plus of inventory when 24-7 first became our partner. Of course, this meant 24-7 got half the profit as well and 40 percent equity, but it was necessary at that time. So that aspect of the partnership was helpful when funds were tight.

Now, however, I can handle things like that myself and keep a close eye on the quality. I am now very knowledgeable on how sourcing overseas works, and I am in control. In effect, with me now taking care of more and more aspects of the business myself, the 24-7 chain has become more or less a silent 40 percent partner. We have learned that if this partnership is going to work, 24-7 needs to just stay out of our way. That way, I can focus on my 9Round family and be very successful. Our relationship today is strictly business, nothing more. The 24-7 mafia knows where they stand, and we know where we stand.

LESSONS LEARNED

For all the negatives, I look at our partnership with 24-7 as a great learning experience. Here at 9Round, we learned the hard way how to do things well. And more importantly, we learned what we *didn't have to do*. Here are some lessons that I learned through this partnership.

- Always maintain operating control. Never, ever, ever give up more than 51 percent of your business, unless you are ready to hand off the reins. Luckily, Heather and I still own 60 percent of 9Round, with no plans to sell in the near future.

- Do your research. And get help. Speak with others in the industry who know your potential business associate. Ask a lawyer to investigate him or her. Look for lawsuits and complaints against either the person or the businesses he or she is part of. Knowing as much as you can will prove invaluable.

- If you are an entrepreneur who becomes involved with a larger outside business entity, you must clearly define the roles of each partner. I only wish I had straightened out the operating agreement before I signed anything with 24-7. Don't think you *have* to have whatever your senior partner wants. The larger business's executives will insist that you are going to need them in order to accomplish this or that. But that may not be true. If you want to create something yourself, you can. Others are going to offer to help you along the way at some point. The bottom line is you really may not need a partner at all. Don't necessarily be starstruck when a bigger, successful company comes along. The 24-7 bigwigs really wowed me at that pivotal meeting up north. Only take a partner if you truly want one, not because that potential partner is bigger and has a fancy headquarters.

- "No, thanks" is a complete sentence. Sometimes saying no can be very hard—especially when someone wealthier who has more experience is in front of you, pushing you to do something you don't feel comfortable with. You have to grow a titanium spine. This one has been a tough one for me because I naturally love to please. But my spine is getting pretty dang tough. Hopefully, your spine hardened up a bit after reading this chapter.

- If you can grow your company without partners, I strongly recommend it. Partnerships can muddy the waters and slow things down. I like to keep my company quick and nimble, so we can turn on a dime. Fortunately,

Heather and I can make all the final decisions swiftly and effectively.

- Don't let glitz and glam sway a decision. When you start having some success, the sharks come out. They will try to court you, impress you, and bribe you. Don't fall for it. Remember the titanium spine?

- I have also learned from this corporate giant how to become a true franchisor. The 24-7 chain did get me in touch with a new law firm to tighten up my franchise agreement. That's a plus.

- I saw how 24-7's real estate department worked (and didn't work). We have adapted some of their tactics and added some of our own. Now we have created the 9Round Real Estate team. We know our brand better than ever before. We know exactly who our customer is and what characteristics the great franchise operators have in common.

- Furthermore, the 24-7 chain incorporated a very nice insurance program for all the individual clubs. Good insurance is a *must* for any business. But even that has had its downside. After it was implemented, we found out that Mr. CEO has an ownership in the insurance company as well. Maddening! Here we go again. I don't mind the 24-7 chain making money, but the company should have at least given me full disclosure of what its CEO has an interest in. No wonder he was pushing the insurance program so hard. Mr. CEO is another great example of the type of businessperson I *do not* want to be.

All in all, being with the 24-7 chain has forced Heather and me to grow, not only as business leaders but also as people. We have learned to trust our gut and to always treat people just like we would like to be treated. That's the Golden Rule, right? Let me tell ya, the 24-7 Golden Rule is "He who has the gold makes the rules." We also learned how much spit and vinegar we have. When we are in the right, we will fight to the death. I think most people would. I believe that sticking to our guns enabled me to fend off the initial fascination and awe of the 24-7 chain and retain control of my own company.

If you have a partner in your business, here is a list of qualities that you will want to have:

1. Transparency/honesty – This is an absolute *must*. Being fully transparent with each other is part of being honest.

2. Absolute 100 percent trust – Once you shake hands (and, of course, button up the partnership on paper), you have to completely trust that each of you will do your part. You can't micromanage each other. If you do that, you will drive each other crazy.

3. Clearly defined roles – You must define what each of you is responsible for, play to your strengths, and stay out of each other's way.

4. Hard work ethic – This one's twofold—(a) know your customer and (b) outwork your competition. Your

partner must understand the customer and the product/ service and must have an equally hard work ethic.

While given what I now know, I likely would have made a different choice about getting involved with the 24-7 chain, but the partnership has had some unexpected benefits. As a result of our collaboration, some of 24-7's sales guys are now working for me. I pay them directly, and the amount is actually a little more than they were earning previously, which of course keeps them happy. Jeff Mathews is still cranking out the sales. He works very hard, he and I are fully transparent with each other, and business is good.

Heather and I really do enjoy developing all these parts of our business ourselves. Hiring new people in the corporate office is just one among the many independent business activities we take joy in doing.

The biggest lesson to draw from all this is that there is no magic bullet—no hocus-pocus, just *focus*. More often than not, the old saying holds true: if you want something done right, do it yourself. Always stick to your guns and trust your gut instinct.

KNOCKOUT NUGGETS

1. *Picking the right partner.* A couple of things I have learned by partnering with the 24-7 chain is what *to do* and what *not to do* when trying to lead an organization. More than ever, I have learned that leading a large organization is all about relationships. To get many people to loyally follow, you must build, nurture, and develop relationships. This is especially true with the people who have bought into your brand. If they think you don't care, then you have lost their trust.

Sometimes being a founder and franchisor of a large company can be a double-edged sword. If a franchisee does great, he or she hardly ever calls me and says, "Shannon, thanks so much!" It's rare that a franchisee says, "Because of you and your team, I have this amazing opportunity." However, if someone's franchise is doing horribly, the first person he or she blames is me and my team. A franchisee who is struggling says, "Corporate doesn't care and doesn't help me." This is a part of the business that Heather and I have had to learn to deal with. All we can do is try our very best to help franchises that aren't doing well as much as we can. If we do that and our heart is in the right place, then we've done all we can do.

But what really makes us feel good about what we do is when we have a franchise owner who listens, executes quickly, and has a wonderful attitude. We are aligned in our thinking, and our goal is to build a brand together. We do have some amazing franchise owners in our company. These are the makers of the world who create jobs and opportunities in this country. In this world there are *makers* and *takers*. I challenge you to become a *maker* today.

2. *Do exactly what you say you are going to do.* That's my father's business philosophy in one simple sentence. And it's the definition of integrity. Remember the honesty lesson above?

I've seen instances in which my father could have made more money on a certain business deal, but because he had already told someone the deal was theirs, he chose to honor his word and take less. This is exactly why my father had great relationships with some of his business friends. He worked with the same guys for twenty or thirty years and in some cases, forty. Too many people talk a good game but don't follow through. My dad has never been one of those people.

Always remember actions speak louder than words. If you have a business partner, show him or her respect by having integrity. If the business doesn't work, then at least you will end the partnership knowing you had integrity throughout the entire relationship. I'm not quite sure that my business partner can say that, but that's their problem, not mine. My integrity is rock solid, and I learned it from my dad.

CHAPTER TEN

KEY PLAYERS

When you start you own brand, it never turns off. Ever! You will now work 24-7-365. At first Heather didn't understand that. But as she got thrown into the business and has taken on more and more, she gets it. Now when I say 24-7-365, I mean you are always thinking about it. You never clock out. You're constantly problem solving.

And that can take a toll on your family life. Heather and I have learned how to separate the business and our family. Family time is sacred time for us, and we take steps to protect it. For example, we don't take phone calls during mealtimes. At certain times of the evening, our focus is on our children, and business issues can wait. Your family situation is different from mine, and you will need to determine how to best set your limits. But whatever those limits look like, you will discover that turning off the business problems will refresh your mind and lead to solutions you hadn't thought of before.

One of the ways we do this is by stacking the phones and iPods at dinner facedown when we are out to eat. If forces us to talk and not be glued to the electronics. Try it!

Because building and running a business is so intensive, you will also find that you have to select good people to help you build your business. Though businesses are often family-oriented and involve family members, the same teamwork principles apply even when you don't have your family in the business with you, as I have. As you build your brand and start your own business, here are some simple tips that will help you work well with others.

1. Define your roles and stay out of each other's way. When Heather, or any other team member, takes on a project, I let that person handle the project, and I just hover at thirty thousand feet. Of course, I let whoever is handling the project know that I am here if he or she needs me. I don't get into the details. I just want to see the results.

2. Communicate often with each other and have weekly meetings. Make the meetings short and to the point. It's easy to be in meeting after meeting and get nothing done. Be sure you have an agenda, stay on task, and get the meeting over quickly so you can get back to building the business. Copy or blind copy your team members on certain e-mails that they need to stay in the loop on.

3. Respect others. Reply to their e-mails and call them back quickly. I instruct my entire team to always respond to me with a 10-4—got it, *on it*! This gives me peace of mind. And now I don't have to ask, "Did you see my e-mail?"

KEY STAFF FOR 9ROUND

My wife is a co-founder, a huge influence on the company, and a fifty-fifty partner both on paper and in reality. Well, actually she's a thirty-thirty partner now. Building 9Round to what it is today meant a grueling schedule for both of us early on. I was killing myself working both mornings and evenings and bouncing back and forth between the karate school and 9Round. In addition to helping with the business, she was, and still is, mother to two children, which God knows is a full-time job in itself. She was thrown into business 101 in a big way, while I grew up always owning my own business and seeing my parents do it. This was all very new to her, and at times, she found it overwhelming.

She is a huge influence on our company and has been involved in all aspects of our business. She has the insight we need to make our main market segment, which is 60–70 percent female, comfortable in the gym. While she leans on me for big-picture guidance, vision, and international development, I lean on her for those areas in which I am weak. So we play to our individual strengths.

Of course, there are a small handful of people besides Heather who have been with us since the beginning of 9Round. These people show what I like to call "fierce loyalty." In fact, loyalty is one of the foundational principles of our company. If I told these core people one day to stand on their heads because the brand would be better off, they wouldn't ask questions, and they would just do it. The first person who comes to mind is Drew Brashier. Drew was one of our early members back in 2008. He still tells the story of how he called up one day and asked about karate training, and I pitched karate and then added that he could try our "little kickboxing thing." After his first karate class, he went over and did a

9Round workout and signed up on the spot. He was hooked. Pun intended.

Drew stayed with the workouts and dropped thirty pounds in three months. Then in early 2009, Heather and I were finally ready to hire our first part-time trainer. She was writing a message on the dry-erase board—part-time help needed—and Drew happened to be there at that time. Talk about good timing, right? Drew immediately perked up. "I would love to work here," he said.

Heather called me and said, "I've found our first trainer." So he was hired.

Today we have over one-thousand trainers in our system, and Drew was the very first one. He has definitely seen it all. Since his first days as a 9Round trainer, Drew has seen all aspects of 9Round and its growth. I remember when I first hired him to work for corporate instead of in the gym. I could only pay him twenty-five thousand a year. He never complained and never asked for more. He just did everything I asked him to do and never questioned anything. He saw the vision that Heather and I saw. Today, we are proud to say that Drew leads the entire franchise support department. He has a big role and a lot of responsibility, and for that, he is one of the highest paid employees of 9Round. Heather and I feel very lucky and proud to have him on our team. He would do anything for the brand, Heather, or me. For that loyalty, he will be rewarded, and Heather and I love giving. That's why we created our company. We not only provide people with better health and fitness, but we can provide jobs and an environment for a person to grow. What a powerful position to be in.

The second person who comes to mind is our IT guy, Jason Bishop. He developed our very first, crappy, one-page website back in 2008. Hey, that's all I could afford at the time. Today, our website has literally thousands of pages and is very complex. In fact, a website is a live being that always has to be tended to. Jason is now in charge of our web developers, SEO (search engine optimization) and SEM (search engine marketing) team, PPC (pay per click) team, and so on. There is always work to do with a growing business. A strong brand has to stay on top of these web developments, and Jason is always on it. He works in the office and from home, and most weeks, I wouldn't be surprised if he puts in sixty hours a week. When there is a major website change, he will pull an all-nighter because that's when there is the least amount of traffic to our site. He's an incredibly smart guy and has a work ethic that rivals mine. He has been a huge asset to Heather, myself, and the entire 9Round organization.

FINDING FRANCHISEES

In an earlier chapter, I told you about our experience with the initial franchisees and how the broker would work with just about anyone who had the money to become a franchisee. Heather and I realized that this strategy was not going to work in the long run, and we were headed down a dead-end road. In fact, I have seen other brands take the route of selling to anybody and, a few years later, having a ton of closed locations. That's exactly what we don't want to happen. Franchise sales is all about the three M's:

1. *Money* – We have to make sure the candidate can financially open and support the business until it is profitable. We've seen owners scrape the money together, and there's nothing wrong with that hustle—the good Lord knows that's what I did—but it puts a huge amount

of stress on the new owner's personal and family life. It makes for an even more challenging start.

2. *Market* – We have to make sure the market is viable. In other words, we have to ask, is there enough disposable income in that area to put a fitness business? At the corporate office, we have strengthened our real estate department and demographic software to be able to quickly figure this out.

3. *Motivation* – The most important factor for me is motivation. Is the candidate in it for the right reasons? Is the potential franchisee passionate about fitness and does he or she really want to help the people of his or her community? It is for this reason that we developed the IST (initial strength test) to weed out the people who aren't truly interested in fitness. Let's be honest; we are in the fitness industry! We got the idea of the IST from the US military.

 The requirements are pretty simple. Each owner must be able to do a mile and a half run in fifteen minutes or less. The males must be able to do fifty push-ups on their toes within two minutes (the females thirty). And the last requirement is that each owner must be able to do fifty sit-ups within a two-minute time period.

 The IST weeds out a lot of investors and people who just have money but no real passion for fitness. This also tells me a lot about the potential owner's character. If he or she passes the test, it reveals a couple of things to me:

 a. He or she was prepared for the test. One of my favorite quotes is "We get paid for preparation."

Another way to say it is "Those who fail to prepare, prepare to fail."

b. He or she takes the requirements and their own personal fitness seriously. You absolutely cannot give what you do not have.

For your business and life, these details will be different, but the ideas are the same. More than ever, I have learned that people will make you very wealthy. They help you create your vision and dream. Get to work on attracting the right people in your life so you can go as high as you can with your dreams.

KNOCKOUT NUGGET

1. *Create mental discipline.* We typically hear a lot about having discipline—always in reference to things like getting up earlier, turning off the TV, exercising, and so on. However, you will become even more powerful if you develop some mental discipline. After all, action always follows thought—meaning thought comes first. In this chapter, I spoke about not being able to "turn it off." That's not always a good thing. Create some downtime so you are not always thinking about your business. Sometimes when I go out to eat with my family or my wife, I leave my cell phone at home. Can you believe that? It's actually a great feeling. I once read a story in *Readers Digest* that had some great advice: "Wherever you are, *be there!*" When you play with your kids, are you 100 percent there? When you are talking to a friend, are you 100 percent there? I challenge you to be in the moment. You will never regret it.

2. *Seek and ye shall find.* I get asked a lot, "How do you find such good people?" The answer is simple. You have to look for them. As the Bible says, "Seek and ye shall find," or, "Ask and ye shall receive." This is especially true when finding good employees or business partners. Let the universe know that you are looking to hire or that you need a savvy business partner. The next step is work hard on seeking. Not only do you have to *ask* and *seek*, but you gotta put in the work. Unfortunately, this is sometimes where people miss the boat. The Bible didn't say, "It's easy."

    Then, of course, know that you will make some mistakes. You will hire the wrong person sometimes or you might have to fire someone, but you can't stop seeking. It's a process, and as with anything in life, if you practice at it, you will get better and better at it. One of the skills that has paid off big-time for me is finding great people. If you are going to build a big business with over one hundred locations, you will have to develop this skill.

3. *We are all creatures of habit.* One of my favorite chants is "Habits we train are habits we gain!" We are all creatures of habit. Over the past five years, Heather and I have created some very good habits in our daily lives. It's a good idea to pick up new habits because it's the small disciplines done daily that will make you a success. A good example is exercise. If you exercise every Monday, Wednesday, and Friday without fail, come rain or shine, you're going to be in pretty good shape. If you take a shower every day, you're going to be clean. If you read and study your craft every day, you will start to

get it and see measurable progress. Here are some great habits to instill in your children at a young age.

- Make your bed. Teaching your child to make his or her own bed will teach him or her to start the day with an accomplishment. If the day is started right, then it's easy to have more things go right.

- Read every night before bed. It's a wonderful idea to teach children that leaders are readers. My son loves to just look at the pictures, but I tell him that the secrets are in the written words. It's so true. If you or your child has trouble reading, you can watch biographies on TV and even listen to an audio program on CD or your iPod. Personally, I learn a lot by listening to audio CDs. It makes my drive time more productive.

- Exercise regularly. Lead by example with your exercise. If a child sees Mommy and Daddy exercising consistently, when that child grows up, he or she will follow suit. Let your kids know that, like bathing, exercise needs to be done regularly. Trust me—you will perform better at everything when you are in good physical condition. Even your love life will be better, if you know what I mean.

- Set goals. Recently, my stepdaughter's soccer coach made the entire team complete a soccer goal-setting worksheet. In fact, the coach said setting the goals was so important that if a team member didn't do it, she couldn't play on the team.

I thought this was fantastic. This exercise forced Elana to write down her goals. Fortunately for her, we had already gone through this with her at the beginning of the year when we routinely make and set our goals. Just making the soccer team was one of her goals that she'd written down, and she made it. Checking off even the smallest goal gives a person a sense of accomplishment and self-confidence.

CHAPTER ELEVEN

GOALS WE SET ARE GOALS WE GET!

We hear so much about setting goals that maybe sometimes we might be tempted to think that the whole concept is overrated. Well, it isn't! That's certainly not the case for me. In fact, I have found that setting goals is essential to success in almost everything important in life. In large part, I have to thank the martial arts for that. After all, when you're advancing through the martial arts, your progress is gauged by ranking and by the belt system. People speak of their ranking with pride. "I am a black belt." "I am a brown belt." But it's the pride of achievement, not of vain boasting. I grew up being guided by that systematic way to approach accomplishments, and it taught me very early to see myself better than I am. It taught me to be visionary.

Setting a goal forces you to look into the future and see what your life would look like if you earned a black belt, a college degree, $1 million, or whatever your heart desires. I feel privileged to have trained under the discipline of the martial arts ever since I was a child. It has always just felt so natural for me. As an adult, the power of consistent discipline has served me well too, in all aspects of life. And that's been especially true when it comes to business and my ambitions as a franchising entrepreneur. My brother made a great quote one time. "It's not about liking it; it's about discipline," he said. That's so true. Do you think I really liked working out twice a day when I was training for my world title fight? Do you really think I loved going to the first forty grand opening celebrations and living out of a suitcase? Heck *no*! I had to sacrifice a lot— especially given that I had a newborn little boy. Boy, did I miss him. What has made me successful is that I am willing to do the things unsuccessful people will not do.

Today when someone asks me, "How do I become successful?" I usually can't tell them everything right then and there. It would be too much for them to take in, and they wouldn't want to hear what it really takes. Let me give you a game plan here. There are four main parts to being successful.

GOAL SETTING (DREAMING)

This is actually fun. There are two types of goals or dreams— short-term and long-term. When I created the 9Round concept, I began with a long-term goal. I began with the end in mind. My long-term goal was to be the largest kickboxing fitness franchise in the world. It was a pretty lofty goal, but remember—Curves had ten thousand locations, so I figured I could get to at least a thousand locations. I had a nice comparison model in my mind.

The second type of goal, the short-term goal, has a twelve-month time frame. My wife and I always make these goals together on January 1 each year. With 9Round, we would set goals such as how much net profit we wanted to achieve, how many locations we wanted to sell, how many locations we wanted to open, and so on. Personally, I set goals like how many times a month or week I wanted to work out, how many books I would read each month, how much money I wanted to save and invest this year, what debts I wanted to pay off this year, and what vacations I wanted to take the family on. As you can see, once you have the big picture and work backward, then it's fairly easy to break the goal down into one-year increments. Then once you have done that, you can break that goal down into even smaller increments, such as thirty days, weekly, or even daily. As the old saying goes, "How do you eat an elephant? One bite at a time." Or said differently, "The journey of one thousand miles begins with a single step."

Look at it this way. Imagine a ship at sea with no captain. Where is it heading? Who knows?! It's wandering around at sea aimlessly, never arriving at a port because it has no idea where the destination is supposed to be in the first place. In other words, it is a ship with no direction. On the other hand, if you have a captain with a compass, then the ship will successfully complete its journey. The captain has set a true course, and he and the crew use the ship's rudder to steer it properly. You are the captain of your own ship, and your goals are your map.

I think parables and analogies help people understand things, and this one needs no further explanation. Goal setting is a great way to avoid procrastination and make sure that you have realistic plans in place for whatever it is that you are trying to accomplish, whether it is for your business or in your personal life. There is something magical about putting a time frame around a goal. I'm not sure how it works, but all I know is that it works. It forces you to get moving. Sometimes you don't have to understand "why"; you just have to trust that it works.

Honestly, I don't understand how electricity works either, but I trust that every time I flip the light switch on, I will have light.

But here's the tricky part: as easy as it is to set goals, it is also very easy not to! It's easy to eat an apple a day, but it's just as easy not to. But if you do, you will benefit from it. The key is to embrace daily disciplines and setting goals. Just make it a part of your routine, along with anything else that propels you forward both in your career and in your personal life. We all know that just a few bad things daily (like overeating, reckless driving, overspending, and the like) can add up and cause absolute disaster. Likewise, if you do a couple of good things a day (exercise, eat right, study new things, and so on) it will, in time, create success. Another good book I recommend reading is *The Compound Effect* by Darren Hardy. Hardy is the publisher of *Success Magazine*, and he does a great job explaining how daily disciplines can create disaster or massive success.

START A BUSINESS!

The second part of being successful is starting a business that creates value. I have never heard, seen, or read about someone who got rich by working for someone else. Create a service or a product that brings value to the marketplace. The way to create wealth is to serve more people. This is the reason Heather and I decided to franchise 9Round. We knew we could reach a lot more people with franchise partners and, in turn, help more people with their fitness, create jobs and opportunities, and help the economy.

Here is a word of advice that I heard a long time ago, and it has really stuck with me: if you don't plan for your future, someone else will. If you think that over a couple of times, you will realize that unless you take your future into your own hands, somebody else—an employer, a boss, or maybe just life's circumstances—will take it into his or her own hands. If you are like me, the type of person who refuses to ever sacrifice his or her independence, early on in life (or maybe later for some) you come to understand that either you're building your own dream or you're helping someone else build theirs. If you don't go ahead and implement your idea, someone else could beat you to it. This is exactly why I implement my ideas very quickly. The more quickly I implement and innovate, the more quickly I know whether or not the idea works.

When it comes to my employees, for example, I genuinely do care about all of them, and I try to help each of them grow as a person. At the end of the day, however, they work for me. They are building my dream.

That is why I think that we are so fortunate that, in this country, we all have an opportunity to strive for entrepreneurship. Now mind you, there is nothing wrong with an honest wage for an honest day's work. And, yes, a salary will earn you a living. But the profits from a business carry the potential to earn you a fortune. As Jim Rohn said, "A wage will earn you a living, but profits will earn you a fortune." As an employee you are going to (hopefully, especially these days) get a raise at the end of the year for hard work, loyalty, and doing a good job. The raise could be 3, 4, or 5 percent, right? Maybe you get a bonus as well? Who knows. But when you create your own business, it is very possible that your income can jump tenfold. Heather and I both experienced this with 9Round. There's no limit to how much profit you can achieve.

If you take a look through history, you will see that the wealthiest people made their fortunes by creating their own business. I want to share with you a list of people who I love to read about and study. This short list can be a great addition to your personal library or a good start if you haven't begun your journey.

Andrew Carnegie – The Scottish American who practically paved the way for the Industrial Revolution, Carnegie pioneered the steel industry with his company Carnegie Steel. After he died, his relatives found a note that he had written. It contained his "life's mission." It said, and I am paraphrasing, that he planned to devote the first half of his life to accumulating as much wealth as he could and the second to giving it all away.

JP Morgan – Morgan invented banking and finance as we know it today. He combined the Edison General Electric Company with the Thomson-Houston Electric Company and formed GE, or what is known today as General Electric. He later even helped finance the United States government. He was a master negotiator and would often merge or consolidate companies to become even more powerful.

John D. Rockefeller – Rockefeller pioneered the oil industry with his company Standard Oil as gasoline and kerosene became more popular. He revolutionized the petroleum industry.

Henry Ford – Creator of a monster of a company called Ford Motor Company, Ford is often credited with inventing the assembly line. His goal was to make it affordable for everyone to own an automobile. With the assembly line and Model T automobile, he revolutionized transportation in America. I like to joke, "I'm the Henry Ford of fitness."

Thomas Edison – This famous inventor held over a thousand patents. He is famous for revolutionary inventions such as the electric light, the phonograph, the light bulb, and the motion picture camera. His products created a ton of value for the world (bringing value to the marketplace).

Sam Walton – The American businessman who opened

Wal-Mart and bought in volume to bring costs down, passing the savings on to the customer, Walton put his stores in small towns, with distribution centers within an hour's drive, so he could keep the shelves stocked with product.

Ray Kroc – This multimixer salesman saw a hamburger stand in California doing gangbusters! Kroc approached the McDonald brothers and struck a deal to duplicate that concept throughout the country. Ray Croc pioneered the franchise industry and fast food. He is one of my idols.

Dave Thomas – The founder of Wendy's fast food, Thomas appeared in more than eight hundred television commercials—more than any other company founder in television history.

Colonel Harland Sanders – Founder of Kentucky Fried Chicken, Sanders started franchising his famous recipe when he was sixty-five years old. Dave Thomas was actually a franchisee of KFC at one time before starting Wendy's. This is an amazing story proving that it's never too late to start your own enterprise.

Tom Monaghan – The story of how Monaghan, founder of Domino's Pizza, created commissaries to keep up with the demand for his pizza is incredible. Monaghan also pioneered delivery pizza—especially with his "delivery in thirty minutes or less or it's *free*" campaign. He was a big fan of keeping things very simple. It took him years to add Diet Coke to the menu because he said it would be another thing owners could screw up.

Richard Branson – Branson is the founder of Virgin Group, which holds over four hundred companies. He is the seventh richest citizen of the United Kingdom, with a net worth of $4.9 billion according to the web.

Donald Trump – Considered to be the most powerful real estate investor and developer in the United States, Trump is a charismatic leader. He also has a hit television show called *The Apprentice*. Heather and I love to watch his show, and when we visit New York City, we always go to Trump Tower. It just gives us inspiration. We always come back from New York City inspired. We are ready to get back in the trenches and get to work.

Robert Kiyosaki – Author of over fifteen books, Kiyosaki teaches financial literacy with his *Rich Dad* products and business. This is the author who got me thinking differently about money, investing, and my direction in life.

Oprah Winfrey – This talk show host/actress is North America's only black billionaire and is probably the most influential woman in the world. Winfrey was born into poverty to a single mother and was raped at age fourteen. She became pregnant, and her infant baby died. Talk about overcoming adversity. What an amazing person!

Howard Schultz – Schultz is the chairman and CEO of Starbucks. A joke has it that they once put a Starbucks inside the bathroom of a Starbucks. They are everywhere.

Steve Jobs – Jobs is co-founder of Apple and a consumer electronics pioneer. His inventions, including the iPod and the iPhone, have changed communication as we know it. I couldn't live without my iPhone. I love it.

Bill Gates – Founder and CEO of Microsoft, the world's largest PC company, Gates is one of the wealthiest men in the world. In fact, his net worth is more than the entire GDP of Iceland according to the Internet.

Mark Zuckerberg – Founder and CEO of the social media phenomenon Facebook, Zuckerberg started this company along with four of his college roommates. His net worth is over $33 billion today.

I enjoy reading and watching biographies on these great

entrepreneurs. If you want to become a wealthy person, study wealthy people and their stories. Here's the interesting thing. Whatever you want to accomplish in your life, someone out there has already achieved it. That is one of the main reasons I wrote this book. I know there are people out there who want to start their own business or have a business and want to expand. Hopefully, they can learn from my experiences and insight.

WORK ON *YOU!*

Jim Rohn said, "Work harder on you, than you do on your job." The third part of becoming a successful anything is personal development. You have to work on yourself and develop the skills and knowledge necessary to be successful. There are two parts to personal development. The first, of course, is your own physical fitness. You can't help the world if you're dead or ill. I challenge you to learn about exercise, health and nutrition, and why getting enough sleep is so important. If you visited my house and looked at my library of books, you would find books on weight lifting, bodybuilding, health and nutrition, and martial arts next to books on real estate and franchising; and alongside these, biographies, history books, and studies of religion and the Bible. And you would find books on success. All these subjects are of interest to me. The second part of personal development is reading and writing things down. Study the books and jot ideas and notes down in your journal. You can't remember everything. Don't trust your memory.

Finally, evaluate your habits. I'm big on the value of positive habits. Be careful about what goes into your mind. Just as a responsible adult doesn't let his or her child watch a movie that is too violent or rated R, we want to stand guard at the gate of our own minds. It is for this reason that I don't watch the local news, read the newspaper, or get caught for an hour on Facebook's news feed. You can't control what other people post, and usually, you see a good bit of negative things. Again, one of my favorite chants is "Habits we train, are habits we gain!"

Another benefit of forming good habits is that you'll have a lot less to think about. You'll get many of things on your to-do list done automatically. There are varied estimates of how long it takes to build a habit (most research says twenty-one days) but the point is that any habit requires repetition to be built. So if you instill good habits into your daily routine, look out! You will now be on a better path. Here are some daily guidelines that I have created to help me build a powerful business:

- Manage the time you spend on e-mail – Be careful here. It's easy to get sucked into e-mails. Hours go by, and nothing has been accomplished. Responding to e-mails all day can pull you away from creating and building your business. Set aside three times a day (say 10:00 a.m., 2:00 p.m., and 6:00 p.m.) during which you are going to sit down and hammer out e-mails. I like to clean my in-box each time. If a guy says, "I'm gonna straighten out this company," but he can't straighten out his e-mails, then there will be problems.

- Be careful not to be a keyboard warrior. It's easy to be a "keyboard warrior" or a "keyboard bully." Remember— once you send that mean e-mail or text message, you can't get it back. Sometimes you can't understand someone's tone with an e-mail or text, so it's best to pick up the phone. If you want to get things done quickly, pick up the dang phone and call whoever you need to call. People are surprised sometimes at how I get quarrels settled very quickly with a simple phone call.

- Get off social media! It's easy to get drawn into the Facebook newsfeed. Before you know it, ten precious minutes are gone, and you are not *any* smarter. It's a complete waste of time. Stand guard at the gate of your mind. Because what goes in always comes out. If you put the good stuff in, good stuff always comes out.

Sometimes it takes listening to someone else to see where the habits we need to change are. Try to set aside a few minutes each day to review your habits and adjust them so you can move in the direction you want to go. Remember—you can't change destinations overnight, but you can change directions.

THE WHITE-HOT DESIRE

The fourth and final piece of the puzzle of being a success can't be taught or learned. It's a burning desire to be a success. Napoleon Hill, who wrote the famous book, *Think and Grow Rich* called it a white-hot desire. He's referring to a flame that burns so hot it looks white. This is what you must have to be a success. From when I was a little boy, I knew I wanted to be wildly successful, and I still strive for that today. I am just as excited on Sunday night as I am on Friday night. I love to work on myself and my business. I love to create miracles each and every day.

FOLLOW THE MAGIC FORMULA FOR SUCCESS

Here's the magic formula for success:

1. *Think big!* – Think really big. Ask yourself, "How can I serve millions of people?"

2. Write down your goals on a sheet of paper or in your journal. Remember—long term is the *big* dream; short term is one year (and even shorter).

3. Bring a value or service to the marketplace by starting a business.

4. Personal development is a *must* – work on your physical fitness, read daily, and write things down.

5. Get a "white-hot desire to be a success! *Go get it!*

KNOCKOUT NUGGETS

1. *Get inspired!* If you want inspiration, all you have to do is shift your mind and start looking for it. It's easy to go around day in and day out just going through life. But if you open your mind and start looking for ideas and inspiration, they will start flying toward you. In fact, I have so many ideas fly through my head every day, I have to write them down, or I will forget them. (Remember—you should never trust your memory.) For me, everything came together—from the decor of 9Round, to the workouts, to the size of the clubs, to the nine stations, to the business model. It didn't happen by accident; it happened because my team and I were looking for it. And today, we are still looking for inspiration to improve the business.

2. *Evolve or die.* Don't be afraid to let your idea evolve. 9Round today is much different from what I first imagined it back in 2008 before we opened, and I'm sure most of the founders I've listed in this chapter would say the same thing about their companies. A great

analogy is your children, if you have any. They are going to grow and evolve as people. They will dress differently than they do now, their hair will be different, and their personality will grow. You have to literally roll with the punches. (Pun intended.) A Greek philosopher once said, "Change is the only constant in life."

One aspect of modern-day business that is constantly changing and that everyone must become used to is technology. If you don't evolve in this area, a competitor could sneak up and pass you. As you evolve personally, you will be able to look into the future with your business eye. These instincts will improve and develop over time.

Life and business are all about the rhythm. Mr. Biggs always teaches this fighting philosophy of the great Sugar Ray Robinson—one of the greatest professional boxers of all time. Sugar Ray would say, "If you control the rhythm, you will control the fight." Life and business have so many similarities to fighting, and rhythm is one of them. You heart beats to a rhythm. Some people's rhythms are faster, and some are slower, but everyone has one. Business also has a rhythm. The economy will go down, and then it will become stronger. Realizing that there are going to be ups and downs and knowing that's normal will put your mind at ease. Remember—if it were easy, everyone would be an entrepreneur. The trick is learning how to deal with the ups and downs.

BONUS INSIGHT: MY DAILY SCHEDULE

7:00 a.m. Time to wake up. Does that surprise you? I bet you thought I got up at 5:00 a.m., downed three raw eggs (like Rocky Balboa), and then went for a three-mile run. Well, I hate to disappoint, but that's not me. I tried the 5:00 a.m.

thing for a while because I'd read about all these successful people getting four or five hours of sleep per night. I quickly learned that if I don't get seven, preferably eight, hours per night, I don't perform at my highest level. You must remember that every day is a performance. You are onstage every day. Whatever you do, figure out how much sleep you need per night to feel and perform at *your* best. The great world champion boxer Sugar Ray Robinson said that rest is a fighter's most valuable weapon.

7:10 a.m. By this time I roll up in the bed. I drink the glass of water I placed on the bedside table right away. I learned this trick from our 9Round nutrition coach, Dr. Rick Kattouf II. He teaches all the members of 9Round that we are dehydrated from the night from the lack of food and sweating. This gets the day started off right. So I recommend *you* drink sixteen ounces of water immediately upon awaking (before coffee).

7:10–7:45 a.m. Time to eat breakfast, get dressed, take the dog up to his outside pen, and get my son, Jackson, ready for school. Heather and I leave the house to take my little man to school. Unless I am traveling, I always go with Heather to drop him off. My wife laughs at me because I have more separation anxiety than Jackson does. I'm the weird parent hanging out the window to tell him bye. I don't care what people think. He's just so special to me. I go to awards day, I go to field day, and I try to eat lunch with him as much as I can at school.

8:00–9:00 a.m. After we get back, my stepdaughter, Elana, is getting ready for her school day. She has to be at school at 8:45 a.m. One of us takes her to school and goes directly to the office from there. Elana is learning to drive in the ninth grade, and sometimes we let her drive to school with one of us in the car. That experience keeps me awake in the morning. All kidding aside, she is doing very well.

9:00 a.m.–6:00 p.m. I am in the office making it rain. I'm in meetings, on the phone, or doing whatever needs to be done to grow the 9Round brand. Sometimes I'm even at our distribution center packing boxes up. A little manual labor never hurt anyone, right?

6:15–8:15 p.m. This is family time. I eat dinner with the family and play with Jackson. We go into the toy room and play an exciting game of kickyball. It's a game we made up, but it's a ton of fun.

8:30–10:00 p.m. I'm back on the computer returning e-mails and preparing for the next day's agenda or reading. I'm always reading something.

10:00–11:00 p.m. I spend time with Heather. We might watch *Shark Tank* or *The Profit* (two of our favorite shows) or just sit on the couch and talk.

11:00 p.m. Lights out.

CHAPTER TWELVE

STORE ONE HUNDRED AND BEYOND

It is truly amazing to discover what a big difference can come from small things. I see other people and other businesses not doing so well, and I find time and time again that it is the simple principles that they *do not* stick to that create the self-imposed barriers to success. It's really not all that difficult to give great service to your customers. Yet it rarely happens! So it is honestly not that surprising that so many businesses fail. Even the fact that I simply do what I say I'm going to do is something that people find refreshing. Well, that baffles me. Being direct, prompt, and honest should just come to you naturally when you are a businessperson.

With this mentality, we opened our one hundredth store on February 10, 2014, in Middleton, Connecticut. I had a local sign maker design a sign that read Our Hundredth Store. Not only was it a significant milestone, but it also served as a great reminder of what you can accomplish, both as a company and as an individual with diligent, steadfast discipline.

You can't let any negativity get to you. Instead, you need to focus and do things the right way in your own organization. Even though I opened one hundred locations in just five short years, my speed was just right for me. Don't let speed dictate quality. If anything, try to learn a lesson from the mistakes that you see others making. Learning from others' mistakes gives me an opportunity to make my organization stand out, by going the extra mile. When I see others doing things the wrong way, I want to make sure I do them the right way. I've done just that with the 24-7 partnership; I can see what the 24-7 franchise does well and what it doesn't do well. I need to make sure my corporate culture is one that my franchisee community feels positive about. I want them to enjoy unlimited success right along with me.

As the franchisor and the proverbial "corporate," I'm, in a sense, the head of a family. As such, it is my obligation (and privilege) to do what is best for the entire family, not just what is best for myself. I need to keep my eye on the big picture. I need to look five years down the line and see what's best for the brand so everyone can benefit.

Some of our franchisees live and breathe 9Round, and they are doing well. The ones who fall off the boat—who, in other words, aren't putting their hearts and souls into their business—don't do nearly as well.

If you have a hundred of anything, you are going to have 10 percent who do great and 10 percent who stink it up, and everyone else is in the middle. That's just life and the law of averages, and it will hold true for franchises as it does for everything else in our world.

Of course, keep in mind how important it is to be passionate about the industry that you're in. I can't overstate how crucial it is to pick the right industry. I could make a lot of money with a McDonald's or Chick-fil-A, but I'm not passionate about that industry. There is no substitute for having a genuine, heartfelt zeal for your business.

My future plans include a thousand stores by the end of 2017. We are all working hard toward that goal. That means the next five years are going to be a grind. I say, "Bring it on!" I'm ready for it, and my staff is too. Yes, I am talking about expanding our business tenfold. My sequel to this book will be *One Hundred to 1,000.*

You have to think *big*! If other brands can do it, so can I. Curves got to ten thousand locations with women alone as their demographic. 9Round is co-ed, so why not? You have to focus on the big picture—which is why my advice is to make the big picture big! At my office, we have a whiteboard that says how many locations we have open. Sometimes I put a number nine in front of our actual number to make it look as if we have nine thousand–plus locations. This simple visualization exercise forces me and my team to think *big*! You can do that same exercise. Make it feel as if you already have the goal you want. For example, when I wanted to win that World Title Kickboxing, I imagined having the belt around my waist. I could feel the weight of the gold on my hips. The feeling part is the secret. Donald Trump said, "If you're gonna dream, dream *big.*" I totally agree!

One of the things that make me equally proud, along with helping people with their health and fitness, is creating jobs and opportunities for others. When Heather and I lay our heads down at night, we know we are giving people opportunities—the opportunity to make a positive impact on their communities, the opportunity to own their own businesses, and the opportunity to make a living for their families and boost the economy. When you get up in the morning and your left foot hits the ground, say to yourself, "Thank," and when your right foot hits, say, "You." Opportunity is everywhere!

If I could leave you with a final thought, it would be this: you don't want to have any regrets. You never want to find yourself saying, "If I had only ..." My personal philosophy is to do everything I do—from kickboxing to business to raising a terrific family—with extreme intensity. I want to be the number one fitness chain in the world. And I know that you can reach the top in your chosen field too. That's the beauty of America. You hold your future right in your own hands.

Open Book Editions
A Berrett-Koehler Partner

Open Book Editions is a joint venture between Berrett-Koehler Publishers and Author Solutions, the market leader in self-publishing. There are many more aspiring authors who share Berrett-Koehler's mission than we can sustainably publish. To serve these authors, Open Book Editions offers a comprehensive self-publishing opportunity.

A Shared Mission

Open Book Editions welcomes authors who share the Berrett-Koehler mission— Creating a World That Works for All. We believe that to truly create a better world, action is needed at all levels—individual, organizational, and societal. At the individual level, our publications help people align their lives with their values and with their aspirations for a better world. At the organizational level, we promote progressive leadership and management practices, socially responsible approaches to business, and humane and effective organizations. At the societal level, we publish content that advances social and economic justice, shared prosperity, sustainability, and new solutions to national and global issues.

Open Book Editions represents a new way to further the BK mission and expand our community. We look forward to helping more authors challenge conventional thinking, introduce new ideas, and foster positive change.

For more information, see the Open Book Editions website:
http://www.iuniverse.com/Packages/OpenBookEditions.aspx

Join the BK Community! See exclusive author videos, join discussion groups, find out about upcoming events, read author blogs, and much more! http://bkcommunity.com/